*Bloom's*

# GUIDES

William Shakespeare's
# Romeo and Juliet
## New Edition

The Adventures of Huckleberry Finn
All the Pretty Horses
Animal Farm
The Autobiography of Malcolm X
The Awakening
The Bell Jar
Beloved
Beowulf
Black Boy
The Bluest Eye
Brave New World
The Canterbury Tales
Catch-22
The Catcher in the Rye
The Chosen
The Crucible
Cry, the Beloved Country
Death of a Salesman
Fahrenheit 451
A Farewell to Arms
Frankenstein
The Glass Menagerie
The Grapes of Wrath
Great Expectations
The Great Gatsby
Hamlet
The Handmaid's Tale
Heart of Darkness
The House on Mango Street
I Know Why the Caged Bird Sings
The Iliad
Invisible Man
Jane Eyre

The Joy Luck Club
The Kite Runner
Lord of the Flies
Macbeth
Maggie: A Girl of the Streets
The Member of the Wedding
The Metamorphosis
Native Son
Night
1984
The Odyssey
Oedipus Rex
Of Mice and Men
One Hundred Years of Solitude
Pride and Prejudice
Ragtime
A Raisin in the Sun
The Red Badge of Courage
Romeo and Juliet
The Scarlet Letter
A Separate Peace
Slaughterhouse-Five
Snow Falling on Cedars
The Stranger
A Streetcar Named Desire
The Sun Also Rises
A Tale of Two Cities
Their Eyes Were Watching God
The Things They Carried
To Kill a Mockingbird
Uncle Tom's Cabin
The Waste Land
Wuthering Heights

*Bloom's*

# GUIDES

William Shakespeare's
# Romeo and Juliet
## New Edition

Edited & with an Introduction
by Harold Bloom

BLOOM'S
LITERARY CRITICISM
*An imprint of Infobase Publishing*

**Bloom's Guides: Romeo and Juliet—New Edition**
Copyright © 2010 by Infobase Publishing
Introduction © 2010 by Harold Bloom

All rights reserved. No part of this book may be reproduced or utilized in any form or by any means, electronic or mechanical, including photocopying, recording, or by any information storage or retrieval systems, without permission in writing from the publisher. For information contact:

Bloom's Literary Criticism
An imprint of Infobase Publishing
132 West 31st Street
New York NY 10001

**Library of Congress Cataloging-in-Publication Data**
William Shakespeare's Romeo and Juliet / edited and with an introduction by Harold Bloom. — New ed.
    p. cm. — (Bloom's guides)
    Includes bibliographical references and index.
    ISBN 978-1-60413-813-9 (hardcover)
    1. Shakespeare, William, 1564–1616. Romeo and Juliet.  2. Tragedy.
    I. Bloom, Harold.   II. Title: Romeo and Juliet.
    PR2831.W55 2010
    822.3'3—dc22                                     2009053107

Bloom's Literary Criticism books are available at special discounts when purchased in bulk quantities for businesses, associations, institutions, or sales promotions. Please call our Special Sales Department in New York at (212) 967–8800 or (800) 322–8755.

You can find Bloom's Literary Criticism on the World Wide Web at http://www.chelseahouse.com

Contributing editor: Portia Williams Weiskel
Cover designed by Takeshi Takahashi
Composition by IBT Global, Troy NY
Cover printed by IBT Global, Troy NY
Book printed and bound by IBT Global, Troy NY
Date printed: May 2010
Printed in the United States of America

10 9 8 7 6 5 4 3 2 1

This book is printed on acid-free paper.

All links and Web addresses were checked and verified to be correct at the time of publication. Because of the dynamic nature of the Web, some addresses and links may have changed since publication and may no longer be valid.

# Contents

# Introduction

HAROLD BLOOM

Harold C. Goddard, in his *The Meaning of Shakespeare* (1951), remarked on how much of Shakespeare turns on the vexed relationships between generations of the same family, which was also one of the burdens of Athenian tragedy. Except for the early *Titus Andronicus*, which I judge to have been a charnel house parody of Christopher Marlowe, *Romeo and Juliet* was Shakespeare's first venture at composing a tragedy and also his first deep investigation of generational perplexities. The Montague-Capulet hatred might seem overwrought enough to have its parodistic aspects, but it destroys two immensely valuable, very young lovers, Juliet of the Capulets and Romeo of the Montagues, and Mercutio as well, a far more interesting character than Romeo. Yet Romeo, exalted by the authentic love between the even more vital Juliet and him, is one of the first instances of the Shakespearean representation of crucial change in a character through self-overhearing and self-reflection. Juliet, an even larger instance, is the play's triumph, since she inaugurates Shakespeare's extraordinary procession of vibrant, life-enhancing women, never matched before or since in all of Western literature, including in Chaucer, who was Shakespeare's truest precursor as the creator of personalities.

Juliet, Mercutio, the nurse, and to a lesser extent Romeo are among the first Shakespearean characters who manifest their author's uncanny genius at inventing persons. Richard III, like Aaron the Moor in *Titus Andronicus*, is a brilliant Marlovian cartoon or grotesque but lacks all inwardness, which is true also of the figures in the earliest comedies. Faulconbridge the Bastard in *King John* and Richard II were Shakespeare's initial breakthroughs in the forging of personalities, before the composition of Romeo and Juliet. After Juliet, Mercutio, and the nurse came Bottom, Shylock, Portia, and most overwhelmingly Falstaff, with whom at last Shakespeare was fully himself. Harold Goddard shrewdly points out that the nurse, who lacks wit, imagination, and above all love, even for Juliet, is no Falstaff, who abounds in cognitive power, creative humor, and (alas) love for the undeserving Hal. The nurse is ferociously lively and funny, but she proves to be exactly what the supremely accurate Juliet eventually calls her: "most wicked fiend," whose care for Juliet has no inward reality. In some sense, the agent of Juliet's tragedy is the nurse, whose failure in loving the child she has raised leads Juliet to the desperate expedient that destroys both Romeo and her.

Mercutio, a superb and delightful role, nevertheless is inwardly quite as cold as the nurse. Though he is Shakespeare's first sketch of a charismatic individual (Berowne in *Love's Labour's Lost* has brilliant language but no charisma), Mercutio is a dangerous companion for Romeo and becomes redundant as soon as Romeo passes from sexual infatuation to sincere love, from Rosaline to Juliet. Age-old directorial wisdom is that Shakespeare killed off Mercutio so quickly because Romeo is a mere stick in contrast to his exuberant friend. But Mercutio becomes irrelevant once Juliet and Romeo fall profoundly in love with each other. What place has Mercutio in the play once it becomes dominated by Juliet's magnificent avowal of her love's infinitude?:

> And yet I wish but for the thing I have.
> My bounty is as boundless as the sea,
> My love as deep; the more I give to thee,
> The more I have, for both are infinite.

Contrast that with Mercutio at his usual bawdy:

> If love be blind, love cannot hit the mark.
> Now will he sit under a medlar tree,
> And wish his mistress were that kind of fruit
> As maids call medlars, when they laugh alone.
> O, Romeo, that she were, O that she were
> An open-arse, thou a pu'rin pear!

Since Juliet develops from strength to strength, Romeo (who is only partly a convert to love) is inevitably dwarfed by her. Partly this is the consequence of what will be Shakespeare's long career of comparing women to men to men's accurate disadvantage, a career that can be said to commence with precisely this play. But partly the tragic flaw is in Romeo himself, who yields too readily to many fierce emotions: anger, fear, grief, and despair. This yielding leads to the death of Tybalt, to Romeo's own suicide, and to Juliet's own farewell to life. Shakespeare is careful to make Romeo just as culpable, in his way, as Mercutio or Tybalt. Juliet, in total contrast, remains radically free of flaw: She is a saint of love, courageous and trusting, refusing the nurse's evil counsel and attempting to hold on to love's truth, which she incarnates. Though it is *The Tragedy of Romeo and Juliet*, the lovers are tragic in wholly different ways. Juliet, in a curious prophecy of Hamlet's charismatic elevation, transcends her self-destruction and dies exalted. Romeo, not of her eminence, dies more pathetically. We are moved by both deaths, but Shakespeare sees to it that our larger loss is the loss of Juliet.

# Biographical Sketch

Although there is a great deal of documentary material (baptismal certificates, marriage licenses, property deeds, mortgages, accounts of law suits, death certificates, a will), of William Shakespeare's actual life little is really known. Whether the man identified as the author of the body of work called Shakespeare's even was the Shakespeare who wrote those works is a question still debated by some.

Shakespeare was baptized on April 26, 1564, in Stratford-on-Avon in England. Traditionally, April 23 is held to be his birthday, for it is St. George's Day (St. George is England's patron saint) and Shakespeare died on April 23 in 1616. Shakespeare's father, John Shakespeare, was a tanner and a glover: He cured animal hides and made them into leather goods like gloves and purses. He was the son of a tenant farmer, Richard Shakespeare, who lived four miles northeast of Stratford in the village of Snitterfield, working for a wealthy landowner, Robert Arden. John Shakespeare married Robert Arden's daughter Mary, and she brought considerable wealth to him. During his first years in Stratford, John Shakespeare grew prosperous and served the town in a number of elected offices including as ale taster, alderman, and high bailiff, or mayor. In 1570, he applied for a coat of arms and for the privilege of writing "Gentleman" after his name. But soon after—it is not known why—his fortune and his public reputation took a turn for the worse. He withdrew his application. In 1580, he had to mortgage his wife's property to pay debts; of the three houses he had once owned, now only one still belonged to him. His name later appears on public records when he was fined for not attending council sessions, not appearing in court, and not attending church.

William Shakespeare was the third of John and Mary's children but the first to survive childhood. He had two brothers—Gilbert, an actor, and Edmund, a haberdasher—who grew into adulthood, although each died young. He gave Gilbert an opulent funeral. His sister, Joan, lived to be seventy-seven, and two of her daughters lived into adulthood and married.

Shakespeare probably went to the Stratford Grammar School. Since his father was an alderman, his tuition would have been waived. According to Nicholas Rowe, his first biographer, writing in 1709, Shakespeare was withdrawn from school in 1678, in order to work, when his father's fortunes began to slide. There are no additional records referring to Shakespeare until November 1682 when his marriage to Anne Hathaway is recorded in the church register in Stratford. The name Hathwey appears on the second entry. Anne Whateley is the name written down when the license is first issued. What is probably an error on the part of an inattentive clerk (the name Whateley appears elsewhere on the same page with regard to other business) has become grounds for much fanciful speculation about Shakespeare's love life.

Anne Hathaway was twenty-six and several months pregnant when they married. She and William settled in his father's house on Henley Street in Stratford. Their first child, Susanna, was christened May 26, 1583. In January 1585, twins, Hamnet and Judith, were born. Hamnet died at the age of eleven in 1596. Judith and Susanna lived into adulthood, married, and had children.

The years between 1585 and 1592 are unaccounted for. It is likely, however, although it cannot be substantiated, that Shakespeare went to London around 1587 with one of the troupes of traveling players that passed through the villages of England. Shakespeare comes back into historical view at the end of 1592 when reference is made to him as a force on the London theater scene by the dramatist Robert Greene in his autobiography *A Groatsworth of Wit*. Greene calls Shakespeare "an upstart crow" who "is as well able to bombast out a blank verse as the best of you," and that "being an absolute Johannes Factotum, is in his own conceit the only Shake-scene in a country." Greene's insult not only reintroduces Shakespeare to the record but served at the time to elicit more information about him. Henry Chettle, who had edited Greene's papers, later apologized, in the preface to his *Kind-Heart's Dream*, for printing Greene's remark. He wrote of Shakespeare that he had personal acquaintance with him and had "seen his demeanor no less civil than he excellent in the quality he professes." Furthermore, Chettle spoke of Shakespeare's "uprightness of dealing, which argues his honesty," and of "his . . . grace in writing."

By 1591, Shakespeare's name was known on the London stage. His *Henry VI* plays had been performed by the Admiral's Company. In the summer of 1592, however, London theaters were closed because of the plague. During this period Shakespeare wrote *Venus and Adonis*, the early sonnets, and *The Rape of Lucrece*. When the theaters reopened in 1594, Shakespeare had joined with several other notable actors of the time, Richard Burbage, John Heminge, Will Kempe, and Henry Condell, to form the Lord Chamberlain's Men. They became the foremost company of the time, performing at the Globe Theater, an outdoor theater, and the Blackfriars, a more exclusive indoor house. They also performed at court for Queen Elizabeth. In 1596, Shakespeare reinstated his father's appeal for a coat of arms, and it was granted. He had a house, New Place, built in Stratford. With the ascendancy of James I, the Lord Chamberlain's Men became His Majesty's Servants, the King's Men. Shakespeare and his fellow actors became Grooms of the Chamber, their revenues increasing, for James demanded many more court performances than Elizabeth had. Beside his career in the theater, Shakespeare also made several real estate investments in London.

Shakespeare was forty-six when he went into semi-retirement. He returned to Stratford but did not stop writing for the London stage and probably traveled between the two towns frequently. At the age of fifty-two he died of what seemed to be a sudden illness. Not long before, he had drawn up his will, bequeathing most of his wealth to his two daughters. We know nothing of his relationship with or his feelings about his wife, Anne. The only bequest he made to her in his will has become famous for its odd and puzzling character. He left her his "second best bed." Perhaps there is no puzzle, however; our best bed is the grave, which affords the truest rest. Any bed in life, compared to that one can be only second best. On the vault of the church over his tomb, Shakespeare had inscribed a plea not to disturb his bones by exhumation.

In 1623, seven years after Shakespeare's death, members of his acting company collected the manuscripts of his plays and printed them in one volume, the First Folio. Within its pages the scanty narrative of Shakespeare's temporal and outer life gives way to the overwhelmingly rich narrative of an inner life that has created for Shakespeare an enduring existence.

The Story Behind the Story

When *Romeo and Juliet* was first published in 1597, the title page of what is now called the first Quarto described it as having been "often (with great applause) plaid publiquely, by the right Ho-/nourable the L. Hunsdon his servants." (Lord Hundson was Queen Elizabeth's Lord Chamberlain and the patron of Shakespeare's acting company.) This allows us to date the composition of the play to around 1595 or 1596. There was no author credited, however. The first attribution of the play to Shakespeare can be found in a 1598 diary entry by a London theatergoer named Francis Meres. The first Quarto is a corrupt text, not copied from Shakespeare's manuscript, but a memorial reconstruction of the play provided to the printer by one of the actors who had performed in it. In 1599, a second Quarto was published. The title page states that it is "Newly corrected, augmented, and amended." It is a far better text, taken from a manuscript close to Shakespeare's original, and it is the one on which all succeeding editions of the play have been based, including the 1623 Folio edition. (A quarto is a volume whose pages are made by folding the paper on which it is printed in four. For a folio, the paper is folded in half.)

The story of Romeo and Juliet was well known in Elizabethan England, and by the time of Shakespeare's play it had appeared in several collections and in various forms. There were versions in two Elizabethan compendia with which Shakespeare was familiar, Belleforest's *Histoires Tragiques* and William Painter's *Palace of Pleasure*. Scholars believe that Shakespeare's primary source, however, is a long poem by Arthur Brooke called *The Tragical Historye of Romeus and Juliet* printed in 1562 and reissued in 1587. In the introduction to his poem, Brooke mentions having seen "the same argument recently set foorth on the stage." In giving the earlier sources of Shakespeare's *Romeo and Juliet*, then, we must realize that they came to him in all likelihood through Brooke's poem.

The story of two lovers resembling Romeo and Juliet, or containing elements of a story similar to theirs, was long a part of continental European literature before it crossed over to England. It has analogs in the stories of Dido and Aeneas, Pyramus and Thisbe, and Troilus and Cressida, all couples whose love is undermined by the social conflicts swirling around them. In the fifth-century A.D. narrative *Ephesiaca*, Xenophon of Ephesus told the story of a wife separated from her husband who avoided marriage to another man by taking a sleeping potion. She, too, awakens in a tomb. In 1476, Masuccio used this motif in a story called "Il Novellino" about Mariotto and Giannozza. They are secretly married by a friar, and Mariotto is exiled after killing someone. Giannozza's father, unaware of his daughter's marriage, plans to marry her to a man of his choosing, and she takes a sleeping potion, escapes from the tomb where she has been interred, and goes to Alexandria, where Mariotto lives in banishment. She is preceded by (the false) news of her death. The messenger to Mariotto, who was to tell him of her scheme and of her impending arrival, is captured and killed by pirates. Mariotto goes to her tomb, is caught, and beheaded. Giannozza dies in a convent.

In 1530, Luigi da Porto took this story as the basis for his *Historia novellamente ritrovata di due nobili amanti*. He set it in Verona and introduced the two feuding families, the Montecchi and the Cappelletti. The lovers are called Romeo and Giulietta. When they meet at a carnival ball, he is suffering from unrequited love, just as Shakespeare's Romeo is. There is no sleeping potion in this version. When Romeo goes to her window to woo her, he mistakes the sleeping Giulietta for dead and kills himself. When she wakes and finds him dead, she kills herself by holding her breath, an element of the story which, fortunately, did not survive this version. Although there is none of the character development that can be found in Shakespeare, a character named Marcuccio, the prototype for Mercutio, is introduced.

In 1554, Matteo Bandello used da Porto's novel as the basis for his own rendition of the story, and five years later, in 1559, Pierre Boaistua translated Bandello's version into French in his *Histoire Tragiques*. From this rendition of the story, Brooke wrote his long poem, which is the immediate source of Shakespeare's play.

List of Characters

**Romeo** is the son of the house of Montague, a wealthy Verona family, and is a young, romantic man. He seems relatively uninvolved in the feud between his family and the Capulets, another wealthy family in the city, and in the course of the play he falls deeply in love with the Capulets' daughter, Juliet. They secretly marry, but events cause Romeo to kill her cousin Tybalt and to be exiled from the city. Upon hearing a false account of Juliet's death, Romeo goes to her tomb and poisons himself.

**Juliet** is the daughter of the house of Capulet, which is engaged in a bloody feud with Romeo's family, the Montagues. Juliet, who at the beginning of the play seems merely a young, naive, and obedient daughter, falls in love with Romeo and marries him. She reveals herself to be tough-minded and courageous when her secret marriage to Romeo is threatened by her father's decision to marry her to Paris. She eventually participates in an elaborate plan to avoid the second marriage by feigning her own death. The plan backfires when Romeo, believing her dead, commits suicide; upon discovering his corpse, Juliet fatally stabs herself.

**Friar Laurence**, a Franciscan monk, performs the secret wedding of Romeo and Juliet and devises the scheme by which Juliet attempts to avoid marrying Paris. The friar is a learned man and offers generally wise advice to a number of other characters; however, the scheme he proposes to Juliet eventually leads to her death and the deaths of Paris and Romeo.

Juliet's **Nurse** is a dedicated and loyal, if somewhat empty-headed, ally of Juliet and plays an important role in getting Romeo and Juliet secretly married. The Nurse's lack of a moral center causes Juliet to discard her as a confidante when she suggests that Juliet marry Paris, despite her existing marriage to Romeo, because Paris is richer.

**Paris**, kin to Prince Escalus and Mercutio, is a wealthy nobleman who wishes to marry Juliet. Although he seems a decent man, he is blind to the fact that Juliet does not care for him and does not want to marry him. He is killed by Romeo, whom he attacks when he thinks Romeo is breaking into the Capulet tomb to defile the bodies.

**Old Capulet** is the head of the Capulet household and Juliet's father. He condones the feud with the Montagues but displays a certain restraint when he prevents Tybalt from attacking Romeo at a party. His character becomes less sympathetic, however, when he attempts to force Juliet to marry the wealthy and powerful Paris. After Romeo and Juliet's suicides, he swears friendship with old Montague.

**Tybalt**, the nephew of Juliet's mother, is an extremely violent and pugnacious young man who kills Romeo's friend Mercutio and is in turn killed by Romeo, causing Romeo to be exiled from Verona.

**Mercutio** is a witty and punning young nobleman and kin to both Paris and Prince Escalus. Although he is not a Montague, he takes their side in the feud, an allegiance that causes him to challenge Tybalt, who kills him.

**Benvolio**, the nephew of old Montague, is a calm and reasonable character who attempts to keep the peace in Verona in the face of an escalating feud.

**Prince Escalus** is the ruler of Verona who exiles Romeo in an attempt to end the Capulet-Montague feud, which he feels is a disturbance and a menace to the citizens of his city.

**Lady Capulet**, Juliet's mother and Tybalt's aunt, encourages Juliet to marry Paris but objects to her husband's abusive behavior when her daughter refuses.

**Old Montague** is head of the Montague household and Romeo's father. He obviously cares for his son but encourages the feud that results in his banishment, which causes Lady Montague to die from grief and ultimately leads to Romeo's suicide.

Summary and Analysis

### I. Conflicts of Will
On the morning of her wedding day to the County Paris, her father's choice of a husband for her, after Juliet's apparently lifeless body is discovered by her nurse, Friar Laurence offers this consolation:

> She's not well married that lives married long,
> But she's best married that dies married young.
>
> IV.v.77f[1]

This is peculiar consolation to give to the parents of a girl who has just died. If it means anything at all, it seems to be an implicit criticism of the institution of marriage and the effect that marriage can have on love. A short marriage, by implication, is better than a long one—perhaps because then the passion of love is frozen in eternity rather than transformed into domesticity. Whether true or not as a critique of marriage or an analysis of love, Friar Laurence's words seem singularly irrelevant under the circumstances.

But Friar Laurence is not actually offering the grieving parents, the bereft bridegroom, and the devoted nurse consolation. And the circumstances are different from what they appear to be to Juliet's mourners. Laurence is only giving the appearance of offering consolation. He is actually scolding them, reproaching them, as the opening lines of his speech clearly show, when he interrupts their keening over Juliet's body:

> Peace ho, for shame! Confusion's [cure] lives not
> In these confusions. Heaven and yourself
> Had part in this fair maid, now heaven hath all,
> And all the better it is for the maid.
>
> IV.v.65ff

Even as Friar Laurence warns against confusion, he is doing his best to maintain their confusion in order to make sure that

18

a scheme that he has devised will both remain hidden and will succeed. He is in league with Juliet to thwart her marriage to Paris and to reunite her with Romeo, already her husband. (Juliet is not, in fact, dead. She has taken a potion the friar has distilled. Its effect is to simulate the appearance of death for twenty-four hours. After Juliet has been interred, Laurence intends for Romeo, secretly returned from banishment in Mantua, to meet her at the tomb and for the lovers, whom he has clandestinely married, to flee to safety.) In consequence, his homily is full of deception. It is all the better for Juliet, as far as he is concerned, to be married to Romeo rather than to be in heaven, as he implies she is, or to be married to Paris, as her parents wish her to be. This is his real and buried meaning.

Laurence scolds the mourners, using conventional Elizabethan rhetoric, for grieving over her death when he argues,

> The most you sought was her promotion,
> For 'twas your heaven she should be advanc'd,
> And weep ye now, seeing she is advanc'd
> Above the clouds, as high as heaven itself?
> O, is this love, you love your child so ill
> That you run mad, seeing that she is well.
>
> IV.v.71ff

This is a common consolation/admonition, often found in Shakespeare's plays (and often, too, spoken in bad faith, as when Claudius, in *Hamlet*, advises Hamlet that his grief for his dead father is excessive, unnatural, and an insult to heaven). Elizabethans said of the dead that they are well. After all, they are in heaven. It is we who are still on earth, alive and subject therefore to mortal suffering, who are ill. But Juliet is not dead though her parents are grieving, and therefore Friar Laurence is deceiving them on two counts; not only is she already married to someone other than Paris, she is not, in Laurence's Elizabethan usage, well, either, since she actually is alive and in the midst of peril largely of their making. When he sermonizes that "She's not well married that lives married long, / But she's best married that dies married young," not only is this a false consolation, but, unbeknownst to him, it is ironically prescient, for that will indeed soon be Juliet's fortune. In addition, he is guilty of the "chopped logic" that not long before had so infuriated Juliet's father.

When Lady Capulet tells Juliet in act 3, scene 5, line 113 that her father has arranged for her to marry Paris, Juliet responds that she "will not marry yet," and continues with an ironic and deceitful equivocation saying, "when I do, I swear / It shall be to Romeo, whom you know I hate, / Rather than Paris." Lady Capulet's "knowledge" is not founded on Juliet's testimony but on her own supposition. Romeo has killed Juliet's cousin, Tybalt, the play's marplot or meddler, and for that reason Romeo has been banished. Romeo's banishment is the cause of Juliet's grief. Since her parents are unaware of their daughter's love for Romeo, however, or of their marriage, which Friar Laurence performed the previous day—on the morning of the afternoon that Romeo killed Tybalt—they reasonably attribute her grief to Tybalt's death and assume that she hates Romeo for killing him. A few lines later, after Lady Capulet has told her husband that Juliet will not consent to marry Paris, Capulet explodes in a series of angry questions:

> Soft, take me with you, take me with you, wife.
> How, will she none? Doth she not give us thanks?
> Is she not proud? Doth she not count her blest,
> Unworthy as she is, that we have wrought
> So worthy a gentleman to be her bride?
>
> III.v.142ff

Juliet responds to him:

> Not proud you have, but thankful that you have.
> Proud can I never be of what I hate,
> But thankful even for hate that is meant love.
>
> III.v.147ff

The way she frames her refusal—with a rhetoric referencing both independence of desire and of judgment, rather than, for example, soliciting her father's understanding or even his mercy, which she could seek without having to reveal her secret—seems to inflame him more than her simple opposition would:

> How, how, how, how, chopped logic! What is this?
> "Proud," and "I thank you," and "I thank you not,"
> And yet "not proud," mistress minion you,
> Thank me no thankings, nor proud me no prouds,
> But fettle your fine joints 'gainst Thursday next,
> To go with Paris to Saint Peter's Church,
> Or I will drag thee on a hurdle thither.
>
> > III.v.150ff

Capulet's passion raised, even Juliet's attempt to soften her speech,

> Good father, I beseech you on my knees,
> Hear me with patience but to speak a word[,]
>
> > III.v.159f

is useless, for he is consumed by his own fire:

> Hang thee, young baggage! Disobedient wretch!
> I tell thee what: get thee to church a' Thursday,
> Or never after look me in the face.
> Speak not, reply not, do not answer me!
> My fingers itch. . . . . . . . . . . . . . . . . . . . . . . . . .
> . . . . . . . . . . . . . . . . . . . . . . I do not use to jest.
> Thursday is near, lay hand on heart, advise.
> And you be mine, I'll give you to my friend;
> And you be not, hang, beg, starve, die in the streets[.]
>
> > III.v.161ff

This blind, violent, and quick temper in him ought to come as no surprise to a reader or spectator of the play. We have seen Capulet's temper flare at act 1, scene 5, line 76, also in a context yoked to Juliet and Romeo's forbidden love, although at both times he is unaware of the connection.

It is at his ball after his nephew, the equally hot-tempered and quick to anger Tybalt, recognizes, by his voice, that one of the maskers is Romeo. Loyal to the feud between the Montagues and the Capulets, whose passionate hatred breaks out sporadically into civic violence, the seething Tybalt informs Capulet,

> Uncle, there is a Montague, our foe;
> A villain that is hither come in spite
> To scorn at our solemnity this night.
>
> I.v.63ff

Capulet notes that it is "young Romeo," and says

> 'A bears him like a portly gentleman;
> And to say truth, Verona brags of him
> To be a virtuous and well-governed youth.
>
> I.v.68ff

But this temperate response is not to Tybalt's liking. He responds, "I'll not endure him," and Capulet, patient at first, fumes,

>      He shall be endured.
> What, goodman boy? I say he shall, go to!
> Am I the master here, or you? go to!
> You'll not endure him! God shall mend my soul
> . . . . . . . . . . . . . . . . . . . . . . go to, go to,
> You are a saucy boy, Is't so indeed?
> This trick may chance to scath you. I know what
> You must contrary me!
>
> I.v.78ff

Here as in the scene with Juliet, Capulet shows that he will brook no challenge to his will. He is ruled by the passion of a violent willfulness. Fundamentally implicit in willfulness is the uncompromising need of the will, of the "I want" to assert itself. This need for self-assertion is characteristic not only of the heightened passion shown by Capulet and Tybalt but of Romeo and Juliet's love also. Characteristic, too, of willfulness is its recklessness, its careening speed. Later, when Romeo demands that Laurence immediately marry him and Juliet— "O, let us hence; I stand on sudden haste"—Friar Laurence warns him (without effect) not to be hasty in the execution of his love, cautioning, "Wisely and slow; they stumble that run fast." In the present instance, at Capulet's ball, the nature of the verse Capulet speaks reflects the psychology of willfulness: The rhyme in his couplet,

> What, goodman boy? I say he shall, go to!
> Am I the master here, or you? go to!

cannot wait for completion and discharges itself at the end of the fourth foot of the second line ("or you?") with its reiteration in the fifth ("go to!") suggesting the uncontrollable haste and repetitiveness of anger. *Romeo and Juliet*, then, ostensibly a story of young love and the obstacles that thwart and frustrate it, is something more than that. It is an exploration of the willfulness of passion and the passionate nature of willfulness. It provides an anatomy of unreflecting self-assertion and offers a sermon, one might say, on the consequences created when the power of human governance rests with the will, whether the will is in the service of amorous or choleric passion.

Shakespeare introduces the theme of will explicitly into *Romeo and Juliet* in act 2, scene 3, when Friar Laurence first appears. It is early morning, and he is roaming the meadows "culling simples," collecting samples of herbs and flowers that he distills into various medicines and potions, like the one he later gives to Juliet to simulate death. As he goes about his labor filling up his "osier cage / With baleful weeds and precious-juiced flowers," he generalizes about the virtues of the plants he is gathering. He begins with a paradox:

The earth that's nature's mother is her tomb;
What is her burying grave that is her womb,

II.iii.9f

and continues, observing that

> . . . from her womb children of divers kind
> We sucking on her natural bosom find,
> Many for many virtues excellent,
> None but for some and yet all different.
> O, mickle is the powerful grace that lies
> In herbs, plants, stones, and their true qualities:
> For nought so vile that on the earth doth live
> But to the earth some special good doth give.

II.iii.11ff

This seems to be an optimistic view of things: There is
nothing, no matter how foul seeming, that does not have
a virtue and cannot be used well. The virtue of a plant,
Laurence observes, is contingent on how it is used, that is, on
the human understanding of nature. Therefore, the opposing
proposition is also true. A plant of good properties can be ill
used:

> Nor aught so good but strain'd from that fair use
> Revolts from true birth, stumbling on abuse:
> Virtue itself turns vice, being misapplied[.]

II.iii.19ff

Laurence gives a specific example from botany to illustrate his
law of contraries and usage:

> Within the infant rind of this small flower
> Poison hath residence and medicine power:
> For this, being smelt, with that part cheers each part;
> Being tasted, slays all senses with the heart.

II.iii.23ff

Friar Laurence then proceeds to moralize his natural science with an application to human psychology and behavior:

> Two such opposed kings encamp them still
> In man as well as herbs, grace and rude will;
> And where the worser is predominant,
> Full soon the canker death eats up that plant.

II.iii.27ff

The exercise of will, Laurence is saying, is like the working of poison. When it governs, death is the result. It is in the realm of one of these kings, "rude will," that the action of *Romeo and Juliet* takes place. The play demonstrates how the working of will subverts and prevents the operation of grace, the unwarranted and unearned, nevertheless manifest gift of heaven's goodness on earth. (For the triumph of grace over will we must wait for Shakespeare's last plays, especially *The Winter's Tale*.)

## II. Between Speech and Deed

The context of *Romeo and Juliet* and the importance of that context are established by the sonnet that serves as the play's prologue:

> Two households, both alike in dignity,
> In fair Verona, where we lay our scene,
> From ancient grudge break to new mutiny,
> Where civil blood makes civil hands unclean.

Prologue, 1ff

Enmity, violence, and disorder are at the heart of the play, and they spring from a grudge. It is an ancient grudge, of whose effects, but not of whose causes, *Romeo and Juliet* is the anatomy. In the play, the grudge itself stands undefined and, for the meaning and drama of the play, uninteresting and unimportant. The only thing we know and need to know about the actual grudge is its generic nature. A grudge is the resentful response to a perceived slight or insult to one's pride or self-interest. The effects of the grudge, on the other hand, are presented in *Romeo and Juliet* with detailed specificity and a Shakespearean realism that, characteristically, discovers and defines the deepest realities of human experience. Moreover, it is the grudge that gives the love between Romeo and Juliet, the radiant kernel of the play, its richness and its resonance. It is within the context of hate-filled enmity, love's contrast, that the love between Romeo and Juliet achieves its intensity. Romantic love, as opposed to domestic or married love, is a rebellion against the social order and its established values, just as it is a rebellion against time and nature, against aging and alteration. (That's why, according to Friar Laurence's puzzling consolation, those individuals are married best who die married young.) In the case of Romeo and Juliet, it is social disorder that stands opposed to their love. Married love can be integrated into society, affirming and continuing it. Romantic love threatens society by asserting an untamed, nonconformist, individual will expressed in passionate desire. Romantic love cannot be integrated into society. Such love must itself be vanquished by the opposition it faces and the lovers must be parted, or it must be tamed into domesticity. If neither of these things happens, if the consecration of the love can be neither the separation of the lovers nor marriage, then it must be death, for it is only the immobility of death that can cheat either society or time and nature.

The sonnet's second quatrain summarizes the plot, emphasizing the reciprocal relationship between love and the grudge:

> From forth the fatal loins of these two foes
> A pair of star-cross'd lovers take their life;
> Whose misadventured piteous overthrows
> Do with their death bury their parents' strife.
>
> Prologue, 5f

With a trick of language, Shakespeare introduces the ambiguity that will serve as an engine of the play and a vehicle for the irony that subverts the process of blossoming and turns it into one of withering. The phrase "lovers take their life" signifies both the processes of birth and of death, presaging Friar Laurence's observation that the earth that is nature's mother is also her tomb. That the "suspense" of the plot is undercut by these four lines suggests that we ought to be looking for something else. This suspicion is confirmed by the final quatrain:

> The fearful passage of their death-mark'd love,
> And the continuance of their parents' rage,
> Which, but their children's end, nought could remove,
> Is now the two hours' traffic of our stage[.]
>
> Prologue, 9ff

By giving away the plot and the ending before the play even begins, Shakespeare is directing our attention elsewhere, not to the unfolding of events but to the psychology of actions, so that we may analyze how it is that such a story can occur, how such events may come to be. Thus in *Romeo and Juliet* Shakespeare moves away from the narrative confines of his sources to a psychological analysis of character and event, probing the source of action.

Shakespeare hurls us into the world of enmity, violence, pride, and vanity in the first scene, as he presents the anatomy of a brawl and explores the psychology of men who become embroiled in it. It is a scene where none of the capacity for ambiguity and mental flexibility required for understanding the opening sonnet can exist. The language of the play now involves quibbles, puns, and posturing, not ambiguity. The characters seem essentially empty and bored were it not for the passion and the poses that their participation in the grudge allows them to counterfeit:

> Sampson: I strike quickly, being moved.
> Gregory: But thou art not quickly moved to strike.
> Sampson: A dog of the house of Montague moves me.
> Gregory: To move is to stir; and to be valiant is to stand:

therefore, if thou art moved, thou runn'st away.
Sampson: A dog of that house shall move me to stand.

I.i.6ff

The scene begins on the streets of Verona where Sampson and Gregory, two of Capulet's servants, are spoiling for a fight, talking tough, bragging sadistically about their sexual prowess and egging each other on until they encounter two of Montague's servants. Quickly the four have exactly what they wanted, something to do that gives them meaning and identity. They exchange taunts and challenges, their swords come out, and they descend on one another. The reason for the brawl exists only in the determination of the brawlers to fight. The conflict, of course, attracts more participants, partisans of both houses and men of higher rank than servants, among them Tybalt, Capulet's nephew. He enters the scene just after Benvolio, of the house of Montague, who has drawn his sword to part the brawlers. In the encounter between the two, Shakespeare shows the force of willfulness and the power passion has over reason. The scene also introduces the kind of dramatic confusion that serves as another of the engines of the plot in *Romeo and Juliet*. Characters such as Tybalt, Mercutio, Capulet, and Romeo and Juliet themselves stubbornly adhere to an overriding passion in order to protect or to justify their positions, their loyalties, their self-conceptions, or their prejudices. The result is a deadly event and a catastrophic consequence:

Benvolio: Part, fools!
Put up your swords; you know not what you do.
[Beats down their swords]
[Enter Tybalt]
Tybalt: What, art thou drawn among these heartless hinds?
Turn thee, Benvolio, look upon thy death.
Benvolio: I do but keep the peace: put up thy sword,
Or manage it to part these men with me.
Tybalt: What, drawn, and talk of peace! I hate the word,
As I hate hell, all Montagues, and thee:
Have at thee, coward!

I.i.66ff

They fight and are joined by others in the brawl, until the two household heads, Capulet and Montague, enter the fray, followed by their wives. Their appearance shows not only the extent and depth of their enmity, but its folly and absurdity. They are each older men whose battling days ought to be behind them, just as Capulet later laments to a cousin at his ball their dancing days are (I.v.33). As Capulet rushes in calling for his sword, his wife restrains him with a reproachful mock, "A crutch, a crutch! why call you for a sword?" (I.i.79). Old Montague's wife is even more adamant as her husband rushes to the fray, physically holding him back, insisting, "Thou shalt not stir a foot to seek a foe," as he cries, "Hold me not, let me go" (I.i.82f).

After the Prince and his municipal guard have restrained the brawlers and restored order, Montague, his wife, and Benvolio are left on the stage. As Old Montague questions Benvolio about how the incident started, Lady Montague interrupts them, changing the focus of the play from the "pernicious rage" of the grudge to her son, Romeo, as she worries about the melancholy gloom that has been afflicting him and causing him to keep himself removed from social interaction. He wanders about Verona's woods sleepless before dawn, and when the morning comes, returns to his darkened room to sleep. At his parents' request, Benvolio promises to find out from Romeo the cause of his melancholy. Old Montague and his wife then withdraw when they see Romeo approaching, and Benvolio greets him.

Benvolio: . . . What sadness lengthens Romeo's hours?
Romeo: Not having that, which, having, makes them short.
Benvolio: In love?
Romeo: Out—
Benvolio: Of love?
Romeo: Out of her favour, where I am in love.
Benvolio: Alas, that love, so gentle in his view,
Should be so tyrannous and rough in proof!
Romeo: Alas, that love, whose view is muffled still,
Should, without eyes, see pathways to his will!
Where shall we dine?

I.i.166ff

The exchange establishes what might be expected. Romeo is in love, stubbornly and willfully in love, and because his love is unrequited, he is tormented both by desire and by the desire to be in love. Yet there are several disconcerting elements. Perhaps not the least is the way Romeo changes key as he asks, "Where shall we dine?" He is apparently emotionally distressed but suffering no loss of appetite. Perhaps his melancholy is less a result of unrequited love than of his will being slighted and the desire to experience romantic passion thwarted. When he complains of his beloved Rosaline's failure to reciprocate his love, his complaint sounds less like a desolate lover's anguish than like the response of petulant will to denial or of a man whose self-determining strategies fail, robbing him of the gratification of victory and pride realized by the construction of a successful identity:

> . . . she'll not be hit
> With Cupid's arrow; she hath Dian's wit;
> And, in strong proof of chastity well arm'd,
> From love's weak childish bow she lives unharm'd.
> She will not stay the siege of loving terms,
> Nor bide the encounter of assailing eyes,
> Nor ope her lap to saint-seducing gold[.]
>
> I.i.211ff

She is frustrating him, while he is complaining. His strategies and his language seem to exist in order to create for himself the identity of a lover rather than either to know, to win, to celebrate or even to lament the loss of his beloved. In one of his lectures on *Romeo and Juliet*, Samuel Taylor Coleridge says of this love that "Rosaline . . . had been a mere name for the yearning of [Romeo's] youthful imagination," that his love for "Rosaline was a mere creation of his fancy; and we should," Coleridge concludes, challenging the authenticity of this love, "remark the boastful positiveness of Romeo in a love of his own making, which is never shown where love is really near the heart."[2] That Romeo's love is motivated in great measure by the will to be in love and to fashion for himself, thereby, an identity ought not to be seen as particularly strange from a historical or a cultural point of view or from the psychological one that Coleridge offers. Romeo is following in a tradition of love and the willful creation of identity that had been developing throughout the Renaissance in such consciousness-shaping writers as Petrarch, Andreas Capelanus, and Baldassare Castiglione. Benjamin Boysen, discussing Petrarch's view of love, explains that "[i]n his Rerum vulgarium fragmenta, Petrarch demonstrates" that

> [l]ove is at one and the same time that which creates his identity, and that which dissolves it anew, it is simultaneously creation and destruction, recognition and alienation, pleasure and suffering—life and death. . . . The project of the poet is monological, and he strives toward a unity with himself, actualized in a circular and narcissistic auto-communication in which he . . . listens to his own speech. . . . He has to express himself in the other in order to appear to himself. . . . He [the poet as conceived by Petrarch] has a strong inclination toward being solitary, unique, independent, and self-enclosed. . . . However, he [Petrarch] often emphasizes that self-consciousness must make the detour by the other, if it is to achieve understanding and consciousness of itself. (*Orbis Litterarum*, vol. 58, no. 3 [June 2003], 163)

The beloved serves to define the lover to himself.

In *The Art of Courtly Love* (ca. 1147), Andreas Capelanus set down the conventions of courtly love, particularly valorizing the condition of being in love. He established the nobility of the lover's worshipful attitude toward his beloved and outlined the rituals of a lover's devotion. Castiglione's *The Courtier* (published in 1528) is a sort of handbook defining how character ought to be formed, what attitudes ought to be developed, which accomplishments are worthy, and how one ought to behave. It was written in the form of a conversation between a group of men and women in which they try to discover what elements are essential to the formation of an ideal identity. Romeo's chief failing as a lover and as a poet when we first see him is his lack of what Castiglione calls *sprezzatura*, the primary requisite of an accomplished person defined as the effortlessness that must characterize everything one does.

Romeo's failure in love, thus, is a failure in self-creation and a frustration of his will. His love of Rosaline shows the strain of an adolescent attempt at the creation of an identity. This failure is particularly apparent in the conventionality of his poetry when we first see him. Love is for the lover an occasion for self-invention through poetry, for the sensuous, inventive linguistic expression of an internal, invisible experience. Romeo's lovelorn state provides him an identity to conceptualize through his speech, and his condition becomes the subject of his poetry. Because it is different from what he wishes it to be, it is full of paradox and oxymoron, as is, according to Petrarch, the nature of love itself as it affects the lover. Romeo's effort is to create an image of himself as lithe and supple in perception and understanding, but the self he is conjuring instead is a defeated one, absorbed in its own failure. Its object, the unresponsive beloved, does not cooperate in his project of self-construction. Construction of a self whose very sense of selfhood is being thwarted is a difficult task for poetry, and Romeo's poetry, at this point in the play, is a failed art. While the sincerity of Romeo's love and of his verse, then, may be open to doubt, the sincerity of his pose can not be. He plays the lover searching in himself for a poetics of love to express himself, and he comes up with the conventional anguish of a rejected lover, reflecting the insincerity of his love rather than the sincerity of his grief:

> Love is a smoke raised with the fume of sighs;
> Being purged, a fire sparkling in lovers' eyes;
> Being vex'd a sea nourish'd with lovers' tears:
> What is it else? a madness most discreet,
> A choking gall and a preserving sweet.

I.i.193ff

This is the sort of thing Shakespeare has had fun with when he's given verse like it to the rustic characters in *As You Like It*. It is also the kind of exercise he will assign to Troilus in *Troilus and Cressida*, who is in love with an image of himself that blinds him to the realities around him in regard to both love or war. We must remember it later on when Romeo meets Juliet and finds authentic and unstrained poetry, needing no bridges like "What is it else?"

The dangerous capacity of language to create or induce belief in a false or self-constructed reality plays a pivotal role in the famous balcony scene between the lovers, when even at the intense height of passionate sincerity, Juliet nearly reproaches Romeo for attempting poetry when he endeavors to convey the strength of his constancy:

> Juliet:. . . . . . . . . . . . . . . . . . . . . .
> Dost thou love me? I know thou wilt say 'Ay,'
> And I will take thy word: yet if thou swear'st,
> Thou mayst prove false; at lovers' perjuries
> They say, Jove laughs. O gentle Romeo,
> If thou dost love, pronounce it faithfully:
> Romeo: Lady, by yonder blessed moon I swear
> That tips with silver all these fruit-tree tops—
> Juliet: O, swear not by the moon, the inconstant moon,
> That monthly changes in her circled orb,
> Lest that thy love prove likewise variable.
> Romeo: What shall I swear by?
> Juliet: Do not swear at all;
> Or, if thou wilt, swear by thy gracious self,
> Which is the god of my idolatry,
> And I'll believe thee.
> Romeo: If my heart's dear love—
> Juliet: Well, do not swear: although I joy in thee,
> I have no joy of this contract to-night:
> It is too rash, too unadvised, too sudden;
> Too like the lightning, which doth cease to be
> Ere one can say 'It lightens.'
>
> II.ii.90ff

The transition from talking about himself and his love to talking about the feud between the Montagues and Capulets is effortless when Romeo notices the aftermath of the brawl as he and Benvolio amble about. The language he uses to consider the enmity, for example, is in the same style as the language he has just used when speaking about himself. His speech essentially is formed of yoked opposites such as "brawling love," "loving hate," "heavy lightness," "serious vanity," "mis-shapen chaos of well-seeming forms," "feather of lead," "bright smoke," "cold fire," "sick health," or "still-waking sleep," oxymora that play with paradox and suggest the identity of opposites. The fight, too, is an opportunity for self-construction, but as a poet, rather than as a partisan combatant. Romeo's initial observation regarding the recent melee—"Here's much to do with hate, but more with love"—is particularly significant just because it is puzzling. Certainly, there is much to do with hate. Hate, however, as interpreted by Romeo's paradox, is the outgrowth of self-love. One needs a hated other to assert his own full identity, just as Romeo needs a beloved to know his, and the love of Juliet and Romeo needs opposition to achieve its full tragic intensity. There is, in the execution of any grudge, much to do with self-love and with nursing injuries or slights to one's sense of self and of self-esteem. Like passionate, sexual, romantic love, hate is fueled by a passion full of self and the one who hates depends on his adversary for his identity as surely as the lover needs the beloved for his own authenticity.

### III. Words as Things

The willful construction of identity through language and the use of language as an indication of will are repeatedly developed in *Romeo and Juliet*, not just in the character of Romeo. The brawling servants of the first scene have no other identities but the ones they express in their allegiances regarding the conflict between the two houses. Capulet's identifying characteristics are his indomitable will and the angry expression of it. Tybalt is entirely defined by "willful choler." It is, however, undoubtedly in the character of Mercutio that Shakespeare most clearly presents both the construction of identity through the construction of a purely linguistic persona and the assertion of a willful identity through language. Dramatically, Mercutio serves as a simple, although decisive, plot device: In act 3, scene 1, his goading engages Tybalt in combat after Romeo has declined to react to Tybalt's provocations, and it is Mercutio's death in that duel with Tybalt, caused more by Romeo's intervention—in an attempt to stop the fight—than by Tybalt's skill, that leads Romeo to kill Tybalt in self-reproachful and vengeful fury. But Mercutio's role and, consequently, his function in the play are far greater than his overt action or his inclusion as a device to propel the plot. He not only embodies the role of language in the creation of character, he is used to provide a linguistic context that serves the construction of psychological texture and depth.

Mercutio, for example, sets the tone of sexual intensity that is implicit in and suggested by the balcony scene in which Romeo and Juliet declare their love. The balcony scene follows quickly after the scene at Capulet's ball, where the lovers first meet. But standing between that scene and the balcony scene are a choral sonnet that introduces the new love and the hindrances it must overcome as well as a scene in which Mercutio and Benvolio search for Romeo, who has gone off on his own at the end of Capulet's ball. Mercutio surmises that Romeo has gone home to bed, but Benvolio says he thinks he saw Romeo scale Capulet's garden wall (which, in fact, is the case) and tells Mercutio, "Call, good Mercutio." Mercutio responds, "Nay, I'll conjure too," mocking at the same time Romeo's pose as a (conventional) lover and poet:

> Romeo! humours! madman! passion! lover!
> Appear thou in the likeness of a sigh:
> Speak but one rhyme, and I am satisfied;
> Cry but 'Ay me!' pronounce but 'love' and 'dove[.]'

II.i.7ff

But Romeo does not appear, and Mercutio, characteristically, continues, enticing him with Rosaline's features:

The ape is dead, and I must conjure him.
I conjure thee by Rosaline's bright eyes,
By her high forehead and her scarlet lip,
By her fine foot, straight leg and quivering thigh[,]

II.i.16ff

Mercutio then mocks these conventional and rarifying phrases with a bawdy turn:

And the demesnes that there adjacent lie.

Benvolio stops him, warning, "if he hear thee, thou wilt anger him," but Mercutio, rather than being halted, uses this admonition as a spur to drive through even riskier linguistic terrain, mined with double entendres.

This cannot anger him: 'twould anger him
To raise a spirit in his mistress' circle
Of some strange nature, letting it there stand
Till she had laid it and conjured it down;
That were some spite: my invocation
Is fair and honest, and in his mistress' name
I conjure only but to raise up him.

II.i.23ff

Thus Mercutio leaves in the reader's or the spectator's mind a sense both of the sexual intensity which is a part of Romeo and Juliet's love and the suggestion of a solely sexual passion, a view that misses entirely the qualities of sanctity, seriousness, and devotion that characterize their love.

Mercutio's most famous speech, however, the Queen Mab speech, seems to have absolutely nothing to do with the action of the play. In that respect, it is unlike his conjuring speech, which provides the bassline against which the melodies and harmonies of the balcony scene play out in contrast to the linguistically gorgeous balcony scene itself. Although the balcony scene is a poetic tour de force, it also constitutes the essential action of the play. Without the poetry of the balcony scene, we would have to take the love between Romeo and Juliet—and its sacredness—on faith, something asserted rather than demonstrated. But by the quality of its poetry, the balcony scene represents materially and sensuously the strength of their love, the force that must overwhelm and propel them, the passion to which they become enslaved.

Mercutio's Queen Mab speech serves partially as an interpretation of dreams. He improvises it on the way to Capulet's party to display his wit. It is woven into the play the way a song is often fitted into a musical. Romeo comments that he has had disturbing dreams, which leads to a witty duel of words between him and Mercutio:

> Romeo: . . . we mean well in going to this mask;
> But 'tis no wit to go.
> Mercutio: Why, may one ask?
> Romeo: I dream'd a dream to-night.
> Mercutio: And so did I.
> Romeo: Well, what was yours?
> Mercutio: That dreamers often lie.
> Romeo: In bed asleep, while they do dream things true.
>
> I.iv.47ff

This dueling exchange in which words change their meanings in a flash culminates in Mercutio's "aria," which begins, "O, then, I see Queen Mab hath been with you." This invention then proceeds for more than forty lines, perhaps producing in the reader or the spectator something of the impatience that helps precipitate the lovers' death. What Mercutio is doing in this speech, however, is turning words into visual imagery in order to convey the working of an invisible force that has the power to create the experience of phantom images. It is just what Shakespeare is doing in the play, which is, after all, showing visible representation of such invisible, intangible, but real forces as love and resentment:

> She is the fairies' midwife, and she comes
> In shape no bigger than an agate-stone
> On the fore-finger of an alderman,
> Drawn with a team of little atomies
> Athwart men's noses as they lie asleep;
> Her wagon-spokes made of long spiders' legs,
> The cover of the wings of grasshoppers,
> The traces of the smallest spider's web,
> The collars of the moonshine's watery beams,
> Her whip of cricket's bone, the lash of film,
> Her wagoner a small grey-coated gnat,
> Not so big as a round little worm
> . . . . . . . . . . . . . . . . . . . . . .
> Her chariot is an empty hazel-nut.
>
> I.iv.54ff

In the Queen Mab speech, Mercutio is representing the miniature world of the fairies, the forces that he fancies activate human desires as they are experienced in dreams through the imaginary stimulation of the various sensory organs:

> . . . . . . . . . . . . . . . . . . . . . . . she gallops night by night
> Through lovers' brains, and then they dream of love;
> O'er courtiers' knees, that dream on court'sies straight,
> O'er lawyers' fingers, who straight dream on fees,
> O'er ladies' lips, who straight on kisses dream,
> . . . . . . . . . . . . . . . . . . . . . . . . . . . . . . .
> Sometime she gallops o'er a courtier's nose,
> And then dreams he of smelling out a suit;
> And sometime comes she with a tithe-pig's tail
> Tickling a parson's nose as a' lies asleep,
> Then dreams, he of another benefice:
> Sometime she driveth o'er a soldier's neck,
> And then dreams he of cutting foreign throats.
>
> I.iv.70ff

As he continues in his speech, however, Mercutio shows Mab as a harbinger of ill-fortune as well as a stimulator of desire, showing a deeper mischief in this figure:

> . . . . . . . . . . . . . . . . . . . . This is that very Mab
> That plats the manes of horses in the night,
> And bakes the elflocks in foul sluttish hairs,
> Which once untangled, much misfortune bodes.
>
> I.iv.88ff

The motif that Friar Laurence will later develop of contradictory capabilities co habiting within a single substance, of the co-presence of birth and death, or of healing and wounding, which we have already encountered in the opening sonnet, is echoed here. Finally, Romeo stops him, crying, "Peace, peace, Mercutio, peace! Thou talk'st of nothing." He admits it readily. "True, I talk of dreams," he says, unthwarted by the interruption, and continues with a riff on a new theme:

> Which are the children of an idle brain,
> Begot of nothing but vain fantasy,
> Which is as thin of substance as the air
> And more inconstant than the wind, who wooes
> Even now the frozen bosom of the north,
> And, being anger'd, puffs away from thence,
> Turning his face to the dew-dropping south.

This time, however, Benvolio stops him with a segue, saying,

> This wind, you talk of, blows us from ourselves;
> Supper is done, and we shall come too late.
>
> I.iv.97ff

But with this innocent riposte, by which Benvolio is simply trying to match Mercutio's wit, Shakespeare makes the language of the play the harbinger of future tragedy, a premonitory allusion to the time when Juliet will wake too late in the tomb to meet not Romeo but death.

## IV. Words as Determinants

When Lady Capulet broaches the subject of marriage with Juliet in act 1, scene 3, she begins with the general question, "How stands your disposition to be married?" It is less a question, however, than an announcement of what is on the agenda for Juliet and what she will be required to conform to it. Juliet answers skillfully: "It is an honor that I dream not of." Juliet's nurse is impressed with the answer:

> An honour! were not I thine only nurse,
> I would say thou hadst suck'd wisdom from thy teat.
>
> I.iii.67f

Why should this reply provoke such a response in the nurse? It is true that the nurse is a figure defined by her vain and comic garrulity, just as Mercutio is defined by his romantic eloquence. Juliet's nurse's long and colorful digression in this scene, however, in which she remembers a fall Juliet took as a child and her husband's bawdy response as well as Juliet's precocious answer, is not merely a comic routine, nor only a painfully comic forecast of the impending tragedy, but an important portrayal of the nurse's character.

> . . . . . . . . . . . . . . . . . . she broke her brow:
> And then my husband—God be with his soul!
> A' was a merry man—took up the child:
> 'Yea,' quoth he, 'dost thou fall upon thy face?
> Thou wilt fall backward when thou hast more wit;
> Wilt thou not, Jule?' and, by my holidame,
> The pretty wretch left crying and said 'Ay.'
> . . . . . . . . . . I never should forget it:
> 'Wilt thou not, Jule?' quoth he;
> And, pretty fool, it stinted and said 'Ay.'
>
> I.iii.38ff

It is the nurse who will serve as the go-between for Romeo and Juliet before they are married, and she will provide them with the conventional machinery of forbidden romance—a rope ladder for Romeo to climb up to Juliet's window, for example—on their marriage night. She is, as her ribald speech suggests, "partly a bawd," and her abandonment of Juliet, when she advises in act 4 that Juliet forget her marriage vows to Romeo and marry Paris, indicate in her a bawd's honor.

In the present circumstance, regarding Juliet's answer to her mother, it is fair to say that the nurse is not being garrulous but recognizes Juliet's gentle diplomacy and charming equivocation—the tactics she will attempt to use so unsuccessfully later with her father—in the face of her mother's subtle but firm manipulation. Juliet's mother is less sympathetic to her daughter's character than the nurse is and sticks to the issue:

> Well, think of marriage now; younger than you,
> Here in Verona, ladies of esteem,
> Are made already mothers: by my count,
> I was your mother much upon these years
> That you are now a maid. Thus then in brief:
> The valiant Paris seeks you for his love.
> . . . . . . . . . .
> What say you? Can you love the gentleman?
> . . . . . . . . . . . . . . . . . . . .
> Speak briefly, can you like of Paris' love?
>
> I.iii.69ff

Characteristically, and evasively, Juliet answers:

> I'll look to like, if looking liking move:
> But no more deep will I endart mine eye
> Than your consent gives strength to make it fly.
>
> I.iii.97ff

This is exactly the tone and the sort of rhetoric that will later so infuriate her father. In this instance, however, her mother does not reproach her subtle and playful mind. She ignores it. This is the way Juliet speaks, and Juliet is not offering opposition to parental authority. She is, in fact, respecting it. "No more deep will [she] endart her eye/ Than [her parents'] consent gives strength to make it fly." As they set out for the festivities, Lady Capulet reminds Juliet that "the County stays," Paris is waiting for her to make her appearance and to make up her mind, too. This last reminder and the tenor of her preceding remarks lend to Lady Capulet's speech a hint of pandering:

> Read o'er the volume of young Paris' face,
> And find delight writ there with beauty's pen;
> Examine every married lineament,
> And see how one another lends content
> And what obscured in this fair volume lies
> Find written in the margent of his eyes.
>
> I.iii.81ff

Although talking specifically about Paris, Lady Capulet has told Juliet that she is now sexually mature, informing her what to look for in men and how to look for it. Lady Capulet is also letting Juliet know that her newly defined power of desire and her newly defined state as a young desirable woman are not to be under her own governance but her parents'. We have heard enough of Juliet already to mark by her language that she is a daughter with a will of her own and a disposition to find and direct her own course. As a rule, daughters in Shakespeare's plays are independent in nature and tend to follow their own prompting, even when it means defiance of their fathers' will. Without intending to, Lady Capulet is preparing Juliet for her meeting with Romeo at the ball.

The encounter between Romeo and Juliet is, foremost, a discovery of a mutual language, and they create the bond of their love by the complicity of their language. Their meeting is a scene of rare delicacy, embedded in the violence that surrounds and will eventually destroy them. We are reminded of their doom by the immediate proximity of Tybalt and his malicious vow of retribution for his uncle's wrath when he expresses his anger at Romeo's presence at Capulet's dance:

Patience perforce with willful choler meeting
Makes my flesh tremble in their different greeting.
I will withdraw: but this intrusion shall
Now seeming sweet convert to bitter gall.

I.v.91ff

When he arrives at Capulet's ball, Romeo is a failed lover, more in love with the melancholy image of himself that failure has engendered than with his presumed beloved, Rosaline. On the way to the ball, as we have seen in discussing Mercutio's Queen Mab speech, Romeo has been bantering with Mercutio, but then he changes the tone of his speech and expresses a foreboding that he cannot explain. The ground is not firm under his feet, but he willfully abandons himself to a devil-may-care recklessness:

. . . my mind misgives
Some consequence yet hanging in the stars
Shall bitterly begin his fearful date
With this night's revels and expire the term
Of a despised life closed in my breast
By some vile forfeit of untimely death.
But He, that hath the steerage of my course,
Direct my sail! On, lusty gentlemen.

I.iv.106ff

This is a pessimistic, almost spiteful surrender to fate, spiteful because he does not believe in the charitable nature of providence.

Shakespeare achieves the sense of the immediate, unifying, passionate, intimate, and playful complicity that characterizes the love between Romeo and Juliet by presenting their first conversation in the form of a sonnet that they spontaneously compose together:

Romeo: If I profane with my unworthiest hand
This holy shrine, the gentle fine is this:

My lips, two blushing pilgrims, ready stand
To smooth that rough touch with a tender kiss.
Juliet: Good pilgrim, you do wrong your hand too much,
Which mannerly devotion shows in this;
For saints have hands that pilgrims' hands do touch,
And palm to palm is holy palmers' kiss.
Romeo: Have not saints lips, and holy palmers too?
Juliet: Ay, pilgrim, lips that they must use in prayer.
Romeo: O, then, dear saint, let lips do what hands do;
They pray, grant thou, lest faith turn to despair.
Juliet: Saints do not move, though grant for prayers' sake.
Romeo: Then move not, while my prayer's effect I take.

I.v.95ff

As the lips join the lovers in a kiss and make them one, more than just symbolically, so the sonnet also joins them making their separate utterance one unified poetic form.

But even as they are becoming one, the forces that will separate them are working around them, framing their love. Just as their sonnet follows directly, as we have seen, on Tybalt's curse, so their dialogue, following that sonnet, is interrupted by Juliet's mother. As Romeo speaks of the kiss they have just exchanged—"Thus from my lips, by yours, my sin is purged," and Juliet responds, "Then have my lips the sin that they have took," which Romeo converts into an opportunity for a second kiss, "Sin from thy lips? O trespass sweetly urged! Give me my sin again," and Juliet teasingly responds, saying, "You kiss by the book,"—Juliet's nurse steps in, telling her, "Madam, your mother craves a word with you."

There are hardly any stage directions in Shakespearean texts, and when there are they are scant, usually only indicating exits and entrances. Consequently, the business around the words on the page, the action one might expect to see on the stage, must be imagined by the reader relying on the text itself, just as it must be derived and blocked from the dialogue by a director for a stage production. In this instance, if there were a stage direction in the text, it would likely read something like,

(Lady Capulet, seeing Juliet flirting with a young man who is not Paris, sends the nurse over to break it up.)
Nurse: Madam, your mother craves a word with you.

Juliet, perhaps blushing, perhaps giving Romeo an exasperated smile or a look of longing and desire, flirts with the young man, and her mother attempts to distract or reprimand her. Romeo then uses this opportunity to ask the nurse, "What [who] is her mother?" and the nurse replies, "Her mother is the lady of the house." "Is she a Capulet?" Romeo says to himself. "O dear account! my life is my foe's debt." A few lines later, as the guests are leaving (and Juliet is no longer having a word with her mother), she asks the nurse to tell her the names of the departing guests. By this ruse she discovers the name of the stranger with whom she exchanged the lines of a sonnet and two kisses.

Go ask his name: if he be married.
My grave is like to be my wedding bed.

Her words sting with irony, for her grave will be her wedding bed precisely because Romeo is not married. The nurse returns and tells her,

His name is Romeo, and a Montague;
The only son of your great enemy.

And Juliet says to herself,

My only love sprung from my only hate!
Too early seen unknown, and known too late!
Prodigious birth of love it is to me,
That I must love a loathed enemy.

I.v.136ff

Embedded in this flowering of love is the problem of what actually constitutes identity, which Juliet proclaims two scenes later from her balcony. Is it the thing itself or the words that point to it?

What's in a name? that which we call a rose
By any other name would smell as sweet[,]

II.ii.43f

Juliet obviously thinks it is the thing itself not the identity
attached to it by disfiguring or falsifying words. Yet for most
of the characters in the play, the words that identify a thing
have become its essential identifier and are thought to be
embodied in it.

### V. Will, Speech, and Control

When Paris first lets Capulet know he would like to marry
Juliet, Capulet's response is neither excessive nor autocratic:

My child is yet a stranger in the world;
She hath not seen the change of fourteen years,
Let two more summers wither in their pride,
Ere we may think her ripe to be a bride.

I.ii.8ff

When Paris presses him, saying, "Younger than she are happy
mothers made," Capulet responds with the caution he himself
later forgets, a caution similar to the warning Friar Laurence
offers Romeo about the dangers of being hasty: "And too
soon marr'd are those so early made." Nevertheless, Capulet
encourages Paris to pursue his hope but adds what, once
again, he will later forget, that his approval depends on Juliet's
acceptance of Paris:

But woo her, gentle Paris, get her heart,
My will to her consent is but a part; An she agree, within her
scope of choice
Lies my consent and fair according voice.

I.ii.16ff

When he abandons his position, the reasons are as unstated
as the reasons for the feud between the houses of Capulet and
Montague. They are never presented and must be inferred—or

dismissed as dramatically irrelevant. What moves the action of the play and creates the drama, conflict, and tension is the decision, one may assert, not the reason for the decision. But the richness of Shakespearean drama results from the depth of character construction, from the portrayal of human authenticity. Shakespeare's characters are alive because they can be moved and determined by thought or feeling that may be hidden from themselves as well as from us. That is why, to use the distinction Erich Auerbach makes in his essay "Odysseus' Scar" in *Mimesis*, the plays can be interpreted as well as analyzed.

In Capulet's case, once asserted, it is clear his will does not bend. When his pride is at stake he is inflexible. It is essential to him to define himself as being in control, and it is second nature to him not to tolerate a challenge to that power. At the time Paris first informs Capulet of his desire to marry Juliet, when Capulet is calm, Capulet's aim is to present himself as a judicious and fair father. Perhaps he is reluctant, without even consciously knowing it, to cede to any man the primacy over Juliet he would lose to her husband, and his temperance cloaks his will to retain possession. He can, in any event, be proud to show his benevolence. His power seems not forced and autocratic but liberal and genial. What then makes Capulet stake his honor on revising that image of himself and presume to say,

> . . . . . . . . . . . I will make a desperate tender
> Of my child's love: I think she will be ruled
> In all respects by me; nay, more, I doubt it not[?]

III.iv.12ff

Why is it "a desperate" offer he makes? He does not explain himself. For the reader or spectator, his words have an eerie and ironic resonance, for unbeknownst to him, he is speaking a terrible truth. He will make a terrible sacrifice of his daughter's love, turning Juliet into a kind of Iphegenia. Although he does not know it, he is giving up his daughter as a sacrificial offering to allay the gods of the feud. Her death will restore social order to Verona, ending the feud between the two houses.

When he says he "thinks she will be ruled / In all respects by me," he is not really "thinking." He is boasting of his power of possession, asserting his own confidence in himself as if saying, "I have faith in my power over her will," and he caps it with a self-congratulatory, "more, I doubt it not." Later, he asserts his sense of ownership of her quite directly in his fit in act 3, scene 5, line 193. (But Juliet's will is no less stark than his, and their encounter proves explosive.) Why does he call his offer desperate if he thinks, however, that Juliet will be ruled by him? The risk, in his mind, cannot be with regard to Juliet, an unconscious premonition of her true nature, but to his own power to be in control, simply to be in control, at a moment when that power of his has been threatened.

> Things have fall'n out, sir, so unluckily,
> That we have had no time to move our daughter:
> Look you, she loved her kinsman Tybalt dearly,
> And so did I:—Well, we were born to die.
>
> III.iv.1ff

His words make it sound like Capulet has accepted the limits of mortality and therefore the limitations of his will: "we were born to die," he says in apparent resignation. But he immediately shows that he has not accepted such limitation. No more than in the scene with Tybalt at the ball or in the scene with Juliet later when Capulet explodes at her refusal to marry Paris has he resigned his will and his need to be in control. Rather, characteristically, when his will is opposed, as we have seen, he defies opposition with a stronger assertion of will. This is what he does in the scene with Paris when he unconditionally offers him Juliet in marriage, bypassing the need to obtain her consent and yoking her desire to his will. Death has momentarily challenged his sense of the power and the finality of his will, and the desperate tender he makes is a bet against death's power. Capulet sacrifices Juliet in a contest with death for the power to be in control of events.

This is clearly evident in act 4, scene 2. Juliet has, for all appearances, capitulated to her father's wishes. She has gone to Friar Laurence's cell, her family thinks, to make confession before her wedding. Really she has gone to plan how she and Romeo will be reunited and to get from Laurence the sleeping potion. Her father, now believing she has abandoned her "self-willed harlotry," is in an affectionate and expansive mood. He is reassured in his possession of her, even as he gives her away, for it is according to his will. He greets her teasingly, alluding to her rebelliousness as if it were a cute misdemeanor, saying: "How now, my headstrong! where have you been gadding?" She replies with seeming openness but full of guile:

Where I have learn'd me to repent the sin
Of disobedient opposition
To you and your behests, and am enjoin'd
By holy Laurence to fall prostrate here,
And beg your pardon: pardon, I beseech you!
Henceforward I am ever ruled by you.

IV.ii.16ff

It is exactly what he wants to hear, especially her promise to be ruled by him forever, and he responds: "Why, I am glad on't; this is well: stand up: / This is as't should be." Notice he does not say, "this is as I want it" but "This is as't should be." He is in control.

Of Capulet, as of King Lear, of whom the former is a foreshadowing figure, it can be said, "he hath ever but slenderly known himself" (*King Lear*, I.i.294). Just as his motives for casting Juliet without her consent onto Paris are not stated, so, it appears, they are not even known to him. Like his daughter and her beloved, he simply is hurtling headlong willfully in the direction his desire propels him, defiant of the overwhelming limitations of mortality. This is what the Greeks meant by hubris, and in this case, it is what makes the tragedy of *Romeo and Juliet* as much the tragedy of Juliet's father as of the lovers.

## VI. The Failure of Words to Change the Course of Things

Once it is set in motion by the meeting of the lovers, the action of *Romeo and Juliet* is swift and hurtles to its climax, despite the many decorative rhetorical and comic flourishes that seem to keep the plot from achieving completion. The action works against the words. The nurse, for example, acting as go-between, strains Juliet's patience by her inability to deliver Romeo's answer quickly regarding when and where they are to meet in order to marry:

> Nurse: I am a-weary, give me leave awhile:
> Fie, how my bones ache! what a jaunt have I had!
> Juliet: I would thou hadst my bones, and I thy news:
> . . . . . . . . . . . . . . . . . . . . . . . . . . . . . . . . . . . . . . . . . .
> Nurse: Jesu, what haste? can you not stay awhile?
> Do you not see that I am out of breath?

Juliet shows the same ability now to distinguish between words and reality in the apparently comic colloquy with the nurse that she displayed when she stopped Romeo, below her window in her father's orchard, from swearing by the moon.

> Juliet: How art thou out of breath, when thou hast breath
> To say to me that thou art out of breath?

But this does not hasten the nurse, who with words creates an image of Romeo for her to savor.

> Nurse: Well, you have made a simple choice; you know not
> how to choose a man: Romeo! no, not he; though his
> face be better than any man's, yet his leg excels
> all men's; and for a hand, and a foot, and a body,
> though they be not to be talked on, yet they are
> past compare: he is not the flower of courtesy,
> but, I'll warrant him, as gentle as a lamb. Go thy
> ways, wench; serve God. What, have you dined at home?
> Juliet: No, no: but all this did I know before.
> What says he of our marriage? what of that?

But the nurse is still not ready, asserting her own need over Juliet's:

> Nurse: Lord, how my head aches! what a head have I!
> It beats as it would fall in twenty pieces.
> My back o' t' other side,—O, my back, my back!
> · · · · · · · · · · · · · · · · · · · · · · · · · · · · · · · · · · · · · · · · · · · · ·
> Juliet: I' faith, I am sorry that thou art not well.
> Sweet, sweet, sweet nurse, tell me, what says my love?
> Nurse: Your love says, like an honest gentleman, and a
> courteous, and a kind, and a handsome, and, I
> warrant, a virtuous,   Where is your mother?
> Juliet: Where is my mother! why, she is within;
> Where should she be? How oddly thou repliest!
> 'Your love says, like an honest gentleman,
> Where is your mother?'

II.v.25ff

The exchange is comic, and it shows how self-indulgent, even willful, the nurse is and how much it comes out in her love of hearing herself talk. The scene also reproduces the tension of impatience, of conflict between the will of an impulse and the resistance it meets. Friar Laurence's speeches also retard the plot as much as they propel it in the long lectures he delivers to Romeo. In the following citation, he is responding to Romeo's disconsolate threat to end his own life after he has been banished from Mantua (and, therefore, Juliet) after killing Tybalt:

> Hold thy desperate hand:. . . . . . . . . . .
> · · · · · · · · · · · · · · · · · · · · · ·
> I thought thy disposition better temper'd.
> Hast thou slain Tybalt? wilt thou slay thyself?
> And slay thy lady too that lives in thee,
> By doing damned hate upon thyself?
> Why rail'st thou on thy birth, the heaven, and earth?
> Since birth, and heaven, and earth, all three do meet
> In thee at once; which thou at once wouldst lose.

Fie, fie, thou shamest thy shape, thy love, thy wit;
Which, like a usurer, abound'st in all,
And usest none in that true use indeed
Which should bedeck thy shape, thy love, thy wit: noble
shape is but a form of wax,
Digressing from the valour of a man;
Thy dear love sworn but hollow perjury,
Killing that love which thou hast vow'd to cherish;
Thy wit, that ornament to shape and love,
Misshapen in the conduct of them both,
Like powder in a skitless soldier's flask,
Is set afire by thine own ignorance,
And thou dismember'd with thine own defence.

Friar Laurence is repeating the theme he introduced in his flower speech: Our virtues and our failings depend on how we use our powers. But the lesson is hardly useful to Romeo, even when Laurence shows him the bright side of things:

What, rouse thee, man! thy Juliet is alive,
For whose dear sake thou wast but lately dead;
There art thou happy: Tybalt would kill thee,
But thou slew'st Tybalt; there are thou happy too:
The law that threaten'd death becomes thy friend
And turns it to exile; there art thou happy:
A pack of blessings lights up upon thy back;
Happiness courts thee in her best array;
But, like a misbehaved and sullen wench,
Thou pout'st upon thy fortune and thy love:
Take heed, take heed, for such die miserable.

It is only when his words become congruent with Romeo's desire that they become effective. Thus, Friar Laurence is not a dispassionate preacher whose allegiance is to the soul's correction. Despite his earlier, insightful words about grace and rude will, he is a chief practitioner of willfulness in *Romeo and Juliet*, intent on shaping the lovers' story to his will despite its apparently destined course, something he realizes too late when he flees from Juliet's tomb in the last act of the play. Now he spurs Romeo on:

> Go, get thee to thy love, as was decreed,
> Ascend her chamber, hence and comfort her:
> But look thou stay not till the watch be set,
> For then thou canst not pass to Mantua;
> Where thou shalt live, till we can find a time
> To blaze your marriage, reconcile your friends,
> Beg pardon of the prince, and call thee back
> With twenty hundred thousand times more joy
> Than thou went'st forth in lamentation.
> Go before, nurse: commend me to thy lady;
> And bid her hasten all the house to bed,
> Which heavy sorrow makes them apt unto:
> Romeo is coming.
>
> III.iii.108ff

For Romeo the lesson is short lived and entirely contingent on apparent circumstance, as his impatient accession to despair when he hears (falsely) of Juliet's death will reveal.

The lovers themselves enjoy idyllic moments together in which time is almost suspended, even as its onrushing force presses against them. The chief source of their trouble is that their love and their will are powerless to alter reality. Not by the stubborn insistence of language nor by the sacrificial devotion of love can they stop the movement of the hours or redefine day and night. Only death can still time.

> Juliet: Wilt thou be gone? it is not yet near day:
> It was the nightingale, and not the lark,
> That pierced the fearful hollow of thine ear;
> . . . . . . . . . . . . . . . . . . . . . . .
> Romeo: It was the lark, the herald of the morn,
> No nightingale: look, love, what envious streaks
> Do lace the severing clouds in yonder east:
> Night's candles are burnt out, and jocund day

Stands tiptoe on the misty mountain tops.
. . . . . . . . . . . . . . . . . . . . . . . . . .
Juliet: Yon light is not day-light, I know it, I:
It is some meteor that the sun exhales,
To be to thee this night a torch-bearer,
And light thee on thy way to Mantua:
Therefore stay yet; thou need'st not to be gone.
Romeo: Let me be ta'en, let me be put to death;
I am content, so thou wilt have it so.
I'll say yon grey is not the morning's eye,
. . . . . . . . . . . . . . . . . . . . . . . . . . . . . . . . . . . . . . . .
Juliet: It is, it is: hie hence, be gone, away!

III.v.1ff

## VII. The Powerlessness of Will

After Friar Laurence gives Juliet the sleeping potion, he writes
to Romeo, banished in Mantua,

> [t]hat he should hither [to Juliet's tomb] come . . . this dire
> night,
> To help to take her from her borrow'd grave,

V.iii.247f

This did not happen because

> . . . he which bore my letter, Friar John,
> Was stay'd by accident, and yesternight
> Return'd my letter back.

V.iii.251ff

The messenger Laurence sent to tell Romeo of the plan to
reunite him and Juliet and spirit them away from Verona under
the guise of death and banishment is prevented from delivering
the information when he is quarantined in a sick man's house.
Thus on the strength of an accident by which human will is
thwarted, the climax of the feud, with its propulsive violence,
is set in motion. Romeo hears only the (false) news that Juliet
is actually dead. In despair and in the sort of haste against

which Laurence earlier warned, Romeo buys a dram of poison from a poor apothecary in Mantua and arrives at Juliet's tomb moments before she awakes and before Laurence arrives to inform her that Romeo has not gotten his message, of which by mischance he himself has just learned. He does not know Romeo is on his way to the tomb with poison to die beside Juliet. His plan having miscarried, Laurence hopes to hide Juliet in his cell, send again for Romeo, and then help the lovers escape. Overwhelmed by the passion of grief, however, Romeo rushes, in frantic despair, longing for death with the same passion with which he longs for Juliet, to the deadly conclusion of the play.

Not only is Romeo unaware of the truth of Juliet's death, he is also unaware of the plans to marry her to Paris, although after he kills Paris in the tomb he recalls that his servant had mentioned it to him but his "betossed soul did not attend him." Romeo is therefore surprised to find a man he does not know, for even as they fight he is unaware that Paris is his opponent, in Juliet's tomb performing rites that clearly, to him, are his own. Paris has come to lay flowers beside the corpse.

> Sweet flower, with flowers thy bridal bed I strew,—
> O woe! thy canopy is dust and stones;—
> Which with sweet water nightly I will dew,
> Or, wanting that, with tears distill'd by moans:
> The obsequies that I for thee will keep
> Nightly shall be to strew thy grave and weep.
>
> V.iii.12ff

Juliet dead serves Paris just as well as Juliet living, perhaps better, for she no longer can frustrate his desire to make her into his image of her. In either case, whether she is alive or dead, it is the idea of possessing Juliet that Paris adores, not Juliet herself, whose own will is of no consequence to him. Throughout the play, Paris courts Juliet only through conversations with her father. There is hardly an indication that Paris and Juliet even know each other. Actual contact between Juliet and Paris occurs only once in *Romeo and Juliet*, over an entirely unromantic twenty lines, when they meet, by accident, at Friar Laurence's cell.

Paris has come to Laurence to arrange the wedding ceremony for his marriage to Juliet. She has come ostensibly to make confession but actually to prevent the marriage and receive the fatal potion from the friar. Their conversation hardly reflects the speech of lovers. It is filled with Juliet's characteristic evasion and equivocation and shows Paris's overconfident will and assumption of formal possession of her. Her words have a different meaning to her from the meaning Paris attributes to them. That Paris is able to remain blind to Juliet's hardly veiled hostility shows he is guided only by his own will:

> Paris: Happily met, my lady and my wife!
> Juliet: That may be, sir, when I may be a wife.
> Paris: That may be must be, love, on Thursday next.
> Juliet: What must be shall be.

Laurence, in a fine display of his own duplicity, interjects what might seem a holy sentiment; but it is really an ironic equivocation that sets him clearly in Juliet's camp:

> Friar Laurence: That's a certain text.

Paris is undaunted by, if he is even cognizant of, Juliet's iciness, and their dialogue continues as it had begun:

> Paris: Come you to make confession to this father?
> Juliet: To answer that, I should confess to you.
> Paris: Do not deny to him that you love me.
> Juliet: I will confess to you that I love him.
> Paris: So will ye, I am sure, that you love me.
> Juliet: If I do so, it will be of more price,
> Being spoke behind your back, than to your face.

Defeated in his attempt at familiarity, Paris tries gentleness, but Juliet is intractable. He again becomes proprietary, and she continues her equivocation:

Paris: Poor soul, thy face is much abused with tears.
Juliet: The tears have got small victory by that;
For it was bad enough before their spite.
Paris: Thou wrong'st it, more than tears, with that report.
Juliet: That is no slander, sir, which is a truth;
And what I spake, I spake it to my face.
Paris: Thy face is mine, and thou hast slander'd it.
Juliet: It may be so, for it is not mine own.

With that hidden rebuff, asserting that her face belongs to Romeo, she turns to Laurence, "Are you at leisure, holy father, now; / Or shall I come to you at evening mass?" saying not another word to Paris, leaving him alone with his unwanted gallantry. When he leaves, instead of saying good-bye to him, she says to Laurence, "O shut the door!" (IV.i.18ff).

Like Romeo at the beginning of the play, Paris in Juliet's tomb is a grieving lover consumed with a passion that feeds on his identity as a frustrated lover. He is interrupted in his lamentation by Romeo's arrival, however. Not knowing any more than what is commonly thought, he thinks that Romeo "here is come to do some villainous shame / To the dead bodies" of Juliet and Tybalt, who is also buried in the tomb of the Capulets.

As he had with Tybalt, so now Romeo tries to avoid Paris's challenge beginning with the words, "Good gentle youth, tempt not a desperate man; / Fly hence, and leave me." Paris, like Tybalt earlier, however, is insistent in his pursuit of what he considers honor and justice. "I do defy thy conjurations, / And apprehend thee for a felon here," he replies. Like Tybalt, too, he is killed by Romeo. The play that had begun with a meaningless brawl and whose change of course or reversal of circumstance was brought on by the vain duel between Tybalt and Mercutio ends with an absurd confrontation fueled by misinformed fury between Romeo and Paris.

Alone after killing Paris, Romeo utters the soliloquy, "How oft when men are at the point of death / Have they been merry!" over Juliet's body as he prepares to take his own life. He is giddy. He wonders why he feels "A lightning before death," when he is going into a realm of darkness. As when he left Juliet's chamber on the morning after their wedding night, the meanings of light and darkness are here reversed. The same paradox occurs: The more brightly lit it became, the deeper the darkness of exile was approaching. The more light he feels now the darker his grief as he endures the darkness of death. But the darkness of death, he notices next, has not descended yet on the corpse of Juliet and extinguished her light. This brings forth in him mortuary poetry—sincere, lovely, and conventional, but subversive, too, of the convention, because it is false. When he asks conventionally,

> Ah, dear Juliet,
> Why art thou yet so fair? shall I believe
> That unsubstantial death is amorous,
> And that the lean abhorred monster keeps
> Thee here in dark to be his paramour?
>
> V.iii.101ff

the ironic answer is because she is alive, not dead. And when he declaims,

> O my love! my wife!
> Death, that hath suck'd the honey of thy breath,
> Hath had no power yet upon thy beauty:
> Thou art not conquer'd; beauty's ensign yet
> Is crimson in thy lips and in thy cheeks,
> And death's pale flag is not advanced there[,]
>
> V.iii.90ff

it is not true because she is not dead. Death will conquer although, as Romeo speaks, its conquest has not yet been accomplished. It is he who now in haste and overwhelmed by the sense of defeated desire has become death's workman.

Although Romeo delivers a long soliloquy before his death, Juliet does not. She speaks directly even if sometimes with equivocation, as we have seen throughout the play, whether to other people or, as in her first soliloquy on her balcony, if the other is not physically present, to herself. She is also not deceitful in her understanding. She analyzes things clearly, and she does not lie to herself, even if she lies to others. She does not try to falsify reality or create an image of herself to her own ideal pleasing. She is not deceived herself when she tries to deceive others, like her father. When she wakes, her mind is clear, "I do remember well where I should be, / And there I am." (V.iii.149f). But things are not as they should be. "Where is my Romeo?" she asks of Friar Laurence who is beside her, having rushed to the tomb. "A greater power than we can contradict / Hath thwarted our intents," (V.iii.153f) he tells her. It is a simple sentence, but it resonates deeply referencing the central theme of the harmful power of will: that a willful act subverts its own desired end.

> Thy husband in thy bosom there lies dead;
> And Paris too. Come, I'll dispose of thee
> Among a sisterhood of holy nuns.
>
> V.iii.155ff

But she refuses to follow. Hearing the noise of the watch approaching, Laurence flees the tomb. Caught in the rush of time and circumstance now, he has actually explained nothing to Juliet. Still she understands well enough, even without knowing the details, just what has happened, "a cup, closed in my true love's hand? Poison, I see, hath been his timeless end." Unreflecting, drawn to Romeo, as she has always been, and as he has been, even when he heard of her death, to her, she hastens after him:

> . . . . . . . . . . . . . . . . . . . . . . I will kiss thy lips;
> Haply some poison yet doth hang on them,
> To make me die with a restorative.
>
> V.iii.161ff

All that is left now is for the participants in the drama who have survived to gather and review the events that led to the catastrophe and to find some resolution. The noise in the tomb has brought the watch, the Prince, Old Montague—his wife has died of grief at Romeo's banishment—the Capulets, Romeo's man, and Paris's. Laurence is brought before them by the watch and quickly tells the story of the play; that retelling of the story serves as its resolution. Grief at their children's death seems to bring the old men to their senses and they end their rift, each embracing the other's loss. For these fathers, death bestows on both the lovers a mythic life as they are metamorphosed from living beings into frozen emblems of love. Rather than a thing of living passion, love becomes symbolic, represented by the golden statue each father will have sculpted of the other's child, not so much to represent the lovers as to represent the reconciliation both men have made with each other. The lovers' integrity of passion is denied them, and they become in death emblems not of their own delight but of their fathers' will to reconciliation.

It remains for the Prince to recall the lovers and the tragic context of their living love. Fittingly for a play about the strength of language and poetry in the construction and assertion of identity, and a play that begins with a sonnet and uses a sonnet to represent the union of two lovers, the Prince ends the play with a recognition of the lovers using the final sestet of his own sonnet:

A glooming peace this morning with it brings;
The sun, for sorrow, will not show his head:
Go hence, to have more talk of these sad things;
Some shall be pardon'd, and some punished:
For never was a story of more woe
Than this of Juliet and her Romeo.

**Notes**

1. This and all other citations from the text refer to: Bryant, J.A., Jr., ed. *The Tragedy of Romeo and Juliet*. New York: New American Library, 1964.

2. http://absoluteshakespeare.com/guides/romeo_and_juliet/essay/romeo_and_juliet_essay.htm

# Critical Views

## A. C. Bradley on Some Elements
of Shakespearean Tragedy

What is the substance of a Shakespearean tragedy, taken in abstraction both from its form and from the differences in point of substance between one tragedy and another? Or thus: What is the nature of the tragic aspect of life as represented by Shakespeare? What is the general fact shown now in this tragedy and now in that? And we are putting the same question when we ask: What is Shakespeare's tragic conception, or conception of tragedy?

These expressions, it should be observed, do not imply that Shakespeare himself ever asked or answered such a question; that he set himself to reflect on the tragic aspects of life, that he framed a tragic conception, and still less that, like Aristotle or Corneille, he had a theory of the kind of poetry called tragedy. These things are all possible; how far any one of them is probable we need not discuss. . . .

A Shakespearean tragedy as so far considered may be called a story of exceptional calamity leading to the death of a man in high estate. But it is clearly much more than this, and we have now to regard it from another side. No amount of calamity which merely befell a man, descending from the clouds like lightning, or stealing from the darkness like pestilence, could alone provide the substance of its story. Job was the greatest of all the children of the east, and his afflictions were well-nigh more than he could bear; but even if we imagined them wearing him to death, that would not make his story tragic. Nor yet would it become so, in the Shakespearean sense, if the fire, and the great wind from the wilderness, and the torments of his flesh were conceived as sent by a supernatural power, whether just or malignant. The calamities of tragedy do not simply happen, nor are they sent; they proceed mainly from actions, and those the actions of men.

We see a number of human beings placed in certain circumstances; and we see, arising from the co-operation of their characters in these circumstances, certain actions. These actions beget others, and these others beget others again, until this series of inter-connected deeds leads by an apparently inevitable sequence to a catastrophe. The effect of such a series on imagination is to make us regard the sufferings which accompany it, and the catastrophe in which it ends, not only or chiefly as something which happens to the persons concerned, but equally as something which is caused by them. This at least may be said of the principal persons, and, among them, of the hero, who always contributes in some measure to the disaster in which he perishes. . . .

[W]hat elements are to be found in the "story" or "action," occasionally or frequently, beside the characteristic deeds, and the sufferings and circumstances, of the persons. I will refer to three of these additional factors.

(a) Shakespeare, occasionally and for reasons which need not be discussed here, represents abnormal conditions of mind; insanity, for example, somnambulism, hallucinations. And deeds issuing from these are certainly not what we called deeds in the fullest sense, deeds expressive of character. No; but these abnormal conditions are never introduced as the origin of deeds of any dramatic moment. Lady Macbeth's sleepwalking has no influence whatever on the events that follow it. Macbeth did not murder Duncan because he saw a dagger in the air: he saw the dagger because he was about to murder Duncan. Lear's insanity is not the cause of a tragic conflict any more than Ophelia's; it is, like Ophelia's, the result of a conflict; and in both cases the effect is mainly pathetic. If Lear were really mad when he divided his kingdom, if Hamlet were really mad at any time in the story, they would cease to be tragic characters.

(b) Shakespeare also introduces the supernatural into some of his tragedies; he introduces ghosts, and witches who have supernatural knowledge. This supernatural element certainly cannot in most cases, if in any, be explained away as an illusion in the mind of one of the characters. And further, it does contribute to the action, and is in more than one instance an indispensable part of it: so that to describe human character, with circumstances, as always the *sole* motive force in this action would be a serious error. But the supernatural is always placed in the closest relation with character. It gives a confirmation and a distinct form to inward movements already present and exerting an influence; to the sense of failure in Brutus to the stifled workings of conscience in Richard, to the half-formed thought or the horrified memory of guilt in Macbeth, to suspicion in Hamlet. Moreover, its influence is never of a compulsive kind. It forms no more than an element, however important, in the problem which the hero has to face; and we are never allowed to feel that it has removed his capacity or responsibility for dealing with this problem. So far indeed are we from feeling this, that many readers run to the opposite extreme, and openly or privately regard the supernatural as having nothing to do with the real interest of the play.

(c) Shakespeare, lastly, in most of his tragedies allows to "chance" or "accident" an appreciable influence at some point in the action. Chance or accident here will be found, I think, to mean any occurrence (not supernatural, of course) which enters the dramatic sequence neither from the agency of a character, nor from the obvious surrounding circumstances.[1] It may be called an accident, in this sense, that Romeo never got the Friar's message about the potion, and that Juliet did not awake from her long sleep a minute sooner; an accident that Edgar arrived at the prison just too late to save Cordelia's life; an accident that Desdemona dropped her handkerchief at the most fatal of moments; an accident that the pirate ship attacked Hamlet's ship, so that he was able to return forthwith to Denmark. Now this operation of accident is a fact, and a prominent fact, of human life. To exclude it *wholly* from tragedy, therefore, would be, we may say, to fail in truth. And, besides, it is not merely a fact. That men may start a course of events but can neither calculate nor control it, is a *tragic* fact. The dramatist may use accident so as to make us feel this; and there are also other dramatic uses to which it may be put. Shakespeare accordingly admits it. On the other hand, any *large* admission of chance into the tragic sequence[2] would certainly weaken, and might destroy, the sense of the causal connection of character, deed, and catastrophe. And Shakespeare really uses it very sparingly. We seldom find ourselves exclaiming, "What an unlucky accident!" I believe most readers would have to search painfully for instances. It is, further, frequently easy to see the dramatic intention of an accident; and some things which look like accidents have really a connection with character, and are therefore not in the full sense accidents. Finally, I believe it will be found that almost all the prominent accidents occur when the action is well advanced and the impression of the causal sequence is too firmly fixed to be impaired.

Thus it appears that these three elements in the "action" are subordinate, while the dominant factor consists in deeds which issue from character. So that, by way of summary, we may now alter our first statement, "A tragedy is a story of exceptional calamity leading to the death of a man in high estate," and we may say instead (what in its turn is one-sided, though less so), that the story is one of human actions producing exceptional calamity and ending in the death of such a man.[3]

### Notes

1. Even a deed would, I think, be counted an "accident," if it were the deed of a very minor person whose character had not been indicated; because such a deed would not issue from the little world to which the dramatist had confined our attention.

2. Comedy stands in a different position. The tricks played by chance often form a principal part of the comic action.

3. It may be observed that the influence of the three elements just considered is to strengthen the tendency, produced by the sufferings considered first, to regard the tragic persons as passive rather than as agents.

## HARRY LEVIN ON FORMALITY AND SPONTANEITY IN SHAKESPEARE'S LANGUAGE OF LOVE

"Fain would I dwell on form—", says Juliet from her window to Romeo in the moonlit orchard below,

Fain would I dwell on form—fain, fain deny
What I have spoke; but farewell compliment! (II.ii.88–89)[1]

Romeo has just violated convention, dramatic and otherwise, by overhearing what Juliet intended to be a soliloquy. Her cousin, Tybalt, had already committed a similar breach of social and theatrical decorum in the scene at the Capulets' feast, where he had also recognized Romeo's voice to be that of a Montague. There, when the lovers first met, the dialogue of their meeting had been formalized into a sonnet, acting out the conceit of his lips as pilgrims, her hand as a shrine, and his kiss as a culminating piece of stage-business, with an encore after an additional quatrain: "You kiss by th' book" (I.v.112). Neither had known the identity of the other; and each, upon finding it out, responded with an ominous exclamation coupling love and death (120, 140). The formality of their encounter was framed by the ceremonious character of the scene, with its dancers, its masquers, and—except for Tybalt's stifled outburst—its air of old-fashioned hospitality. "We'll measure them a measure", Benvolio had proposed; but Romeo, unwilling to join the dance, had resolved to be an onlooker and carry a torch (I.iv.10). That torch may have burned symbolically, but not for Juliet; indeed, as we are inclined to forget with Romeo, he attended the feast in order to see the dazzling but soon eclipsed Rosaline. Rosaline's prior effect upon him is all that we ever learn about her; yet it has been enough to make Romeo, when he was presented to us, a virtual stereotype of the romantic lover. As such, he has protested a good deal too much in his preliminary speeches, utilizing the conventional phrases and standardized images of Elizabethan eroticism, bandying generalizations, paradoxes, and sestets with Benvolio, and taking a quasi-religious vow which his introduction to Juliet would ironically break (I.ii.92–97). Afterward this role has been reduced to absurdity by the humorous man, Mercutio, in a mock-conjuration evoking Venus and Cupid and the inevitable jingle of "love" and "dove" (II.i.10). The scene that follows is actually a continuation, marked in neither the Folios nor the Quartos, and linked with what has gone before by a somewhat eroded rhyme.

> 'Tis in vain
> To seek him here that means not to be found,

Benvolio concludes in the absence of Romeo (41, 42). Whereupon the latter, on the other side of the wall, chimes in:

> He jests at scars that never felt a wound. (II.ii.1)

Thus we stay behind, with Romeo, when the masquers depart. Juliet, appearing at the window, does not hear his descriptive invocation. Her first utterance is the very sigh that Mercutio burlesqued in the foregoing scene: "Ay, me!" (II.ii.25). Then, believing herself to be alone and masked by the darkness, she speaks her mind in sincerity and simplicity. She calls into question not merely Romeo's name but—by implication— all names, forms, conventions, sophistications, and arbitrary dictates of society, as opposed to the appeal of instinct directly conveyed in the odor of a rose. When Romeo takes her at her word and answers, she is startled and even alarmed for his sake; but she does not revert to courtly language.

> I would not for the world they saw thee here,

she tells him, and her monosyllabic directness inspires the matching cadence of his response:

> And but thou love me, let them find me here. (77, 79)

She pays incidental tribute to the proprieties with her passing suggestion that, had he not overheard her, she would have dwelt on form, pretended to be more distant, and played the not impossible part of the captious beloved. But farewell compliment! Romeo's love for Juliet will have an immediacy which cuts straight through the verbal embellishment that has obscured his infatuation with Rosaline. That shadowy creature, having served her Dulcinea-like purpose, may well be forgotten. On the other hand, Romeo has his more tangible foil in the person of the County Paris, who is cast in that ungrateful part which the Italians call *terzo incòmodo*, the inconvenient third party, the unwelcome member of an amorous triangle. As the official suitor of Juliet, his speeches are always formal, and often sound stilted or priggish by contrast with Romeo's. Long after Romeo has abandoned his sonneteering, Paris will pronounce a sestet at Juliet's tomb (V.iii.11–16). During their only colloquy, which occurs in Friar Laurence's cell, Juliet takes on the sophisticated tone of Paris, denying his claims and disclaiming his compliments in brisk stichomythy. As soon as he leaves, she turns to the Friar, and again—as so often in intimate moments—her lines fall into monosyllables:

O, shut the door! and when thou hast done so,
Come weep with me—past hope, past cure, past help! (IV. i.44–45)

Since the suit of Paris is the main subject of her conversations with her parents, she can hardly be sincere with them. Even before she met Romeo, her consent was hedged in prim phraseology:

I'll look to like, if looking liking move. (I.iii.97)

And after her involvement she becomes adept in the strategems of mental reservation, giving her mother equivocal rejoinders and rousing her father's anger by chopping logic (III.v.69–205). Despite the intervention of the Nurse on her behalf, her one straightforward plea is disregarded. Significantly Lady Capulet, broaching the theme of Paris in stiffly appropriate couplets, has compared his face to a volume:[2]

This precious book of love, this unbound lover,
To beautify him only lacks a cover.
The fish lives in the sea, and 'tis much pride
The fair without the fair within to hide. (I.iii.89–90)

That bookish comparison, by emphasizing the letter at the expense of the spirit, helps to lend Paris an aspect of unreality;

to the Nurse, more ingenuously, he is "a man of wax" (76). Later Juliet will echo Lady Capulet's metaphor, transferring it from Paris to Romeo:

> Was ever book containing such vile matter
> So fairly bound? (III.ii.83–84)

Here, on having learned that Romeo has just slain Tybalt, she is undergoing a crisis of doubt, a typically Shakespearian recognition of the difference between appearance and reality. The fair without may not cover a fair within, after all. Her unjustified accusations, leading up to her rhetorical question, form a sequence of oxymoronic epithets: "Beautiful tyrant, fiend angelical, . . . honorable villain!" (75–79) W. H. Auden, in a recent comment on these lines,[3] cannot believe they would come from a heroine who had been exclaiming shortly before: "Gallop apace, you fiery-footed steeds . . . !" Yet Shakespeare has been perfectly consistent in suiting changes of style to changes of mood. When Juliet feels at one with Romeo, her intonations are genuine; when she feels at odds with him, they should be unconvincing. The attraction of love is played off against the revulsion from books, and coupled with the closely related themes of youth and haste, in one of Romeo's long-drawn-out leavetakings:

> Love goes toward love as schoolboys from their books;
> But love from love, towards school with heavy looks.
> (II.ii.157–158)[3]

The school for these young lovers will be tragic experience. When Romeo, assuming that Juliet is dead and contemplating his own death, recognizes the corpse of Paris, he will extend the image to cover them both:

> O give me thy hand,
> One writ with me in sour misfortune's book! (V.iii.82)

It was this recoil from bookishness, together with the farewell to compliment, that animated *Love's Labour's Lost*, where literary artifice was so ingeniously deployed against itself, and Berowne was taught—by an actual heroine named Rosaline—that the best books were women's eyes. Some of Shakespeare's other early comedies came even closer to adumbrating certain features of *Romeo and Juliet*: notably, *The Two Gentlemen of Verona*, with its locale, its window scene, its friar and rope, its betrothal and banishment, its emphasis upon the vagaries of love. Shakespeare's sonnets and erotic poems had won for him the reputation of an English Ovid. *Romeo and Juliet*, the most elaborate product of his so-called lyrical period, was his first successful experiment in tragedy.[4] Because of that very success, it is hard for us to realize the full extent of its novelty, though scholarship has lately been reminding us of how it must have struck contemporaries.[5] They would have been surprised, and possibly shocked, at seeing lovers taken so seriously. Legend, it had been heretofore taken for granted, was the proper matter for serious drama; romance was the stuff of the comic stage. Romantic tragedy—"*an excellent conceited Tragedie of Romeo and Juliet*", to cite the title-page of the First Quarto—was one of those contradictions in terms which Shakespeare seems to have delighted in resolving. His innovation might be described as transcending the usages of romantic comedy, which are therefore very much in evidence, particularly at the beginning. Subsequently, the leading characters acquire together a deeper dimension of feeling by expressly repudiating the artificial language they have talked and the superficial code they have lived by. Their formula might be that of the anti-Petrarchan sonnet:

Foole said My muse to mee, looke in thy heart and write.[6]

### Notes

1. Line references are to the separate edition of G. L. Kittredge's text (Boston, 1940).

2. On the long and rich history of this trope, see the sixteenth chapter of E. R. Curtius, *European Literature and the Latin Middle Ages*, tr. W. R. Trask (New York, 1953).

3. In the paper-bound Laurel Shakespeare, ed. Francis Fergusson (New York, 1958), p. 26.

4. H. B. Charlton, in his British Academy lecture for 1939, *"Romeo and Juliet" as an Experimental Tragedy*, has considered the experiment in the light of Renaissance critical theory.

5. Especially F. M. Dickey, *Not Wisely But Too Well: Shakespeare's Love Tragedies* (San Marino, 1957), pp. 63–88.

6. Sir Philip Sidney, *Astrophel and Stella*, ed. Albert Feuillerat (Cambridge, 1922), p. 243.

## Sara Munson Deats on Isolation, Miscommunication, and Adolescent Suicide in the Play

In Tampa, Florida, in 1986, a high school teacher contacted the local suicide crisis center before teaching *Romeo and Juliet* and asked for advice in treating the play's delicate subject matter with her students. . . . In the same year, a psychologist at a Tampa high school where a young man had recently committed suicide in the classroom contacted a university English professor and requested guidance in teaching *Romeo and Juliet* for the English faculty. . . . That year in Washington, DC, the Shakespeare Theatre at the Folger Shakespeare Library and the Youth Suicide National Center collaborated to create a program intended to "enable teenagers to experience the high drama of Shakespeare's classic, and, at the same time, to understand its relevance to their lives" (Holmer, "Pedagogical Practices" 192).

These . . . incidents . . . reinforce my conviction that *Romeo and Juliet*, one of our culture's most cherished love stories and the culture's most celebrated dramatization of teenage suicide, has a special resonance for young people today. I find this play significant not because Shakespeare is a writer for all times or because this tragedy embodies essential, universal insights but because in this drama, as in many of his works, Shakespeare brilliantly synthesizes the traditions and customs from which our contemporary mores have evolved. Thus, despite the enormous technological advances and monumental social changes that have occurred during the past four hundred years, the problems confronting Romeo and Juliet—the tensions between parents and children in the nuclear patriarchal family, the pressures within masculine peer groups, and the failure of authority figures to mediate between young people and the establishment—are still a part of our culture. . . .

Throughout the centuries, this popular and provocative play has evoked a multitude of interpretations. Commentators have read the play as a tragedy of fate and the stars . . . a tragedy of haste . . . a tragedy of excessive passion . . . a tragedy of unawareness . . . , a tragedy of violated ritual . . . and the locus classicus of the *Liebestod* myth. . . . Other critics have focused on the conflicts of the individual versus the patriarchy . . . love versus friendship . . . and subversion versus tradition. . . . Several intriguing interpretations of the play present *Romeo and Juliet* as a dramatic oxymoron, a study in contrarieties—love and death, age and youth, high and low spheres, authority and rebellion, love and hate, comedy and tragedy. . . . To this list of antinomies, I would add the frequently overlooked polarities of communication and alienation, since this play showcases some of Shakespeare's most dazzling rhetoric while dramatizing a radical breakdown in communication on all levels of Verona society. This aspect of the play, enacting a dilemma as old as a cuneiform chronicle yet as current as the six o'clock news, is particularly relevant to the contemporary epidemic of teenage suicide.

The collapse of communication pervades the society of the play. First, and most crucially, parents and children cannot relate to each other; as most of us are aware, *Romeo and Juliet* is one of the definitive treatments in literature of the generation gap. . . . Second, and not so frequently recognized, Veronese society's masculine peer group cannot establish a frank and open dialogue. Lastly, societal institutions—the state and the church—are unable to maintain order or mediate between the estranged parents and their children. Ultimately, Romeo and Juliet, alienated from both family and peers, make a total, exclusive commitment to each other while appealing to the church for solace and aid. When the church, in the persona of the bumbling, pusillanimous Friar Laurence, fails them, they cling desperately to each other. Even this support collapses, and each lover, believing the other to be dead, feels isolated and abandoned and sees no recourse but suicide.

The introductions of both teenagers stress the psychic gulf separating parents and children in Verona. Although Juliet makes her debut flanked by her mother and her nurse, Lady Capulet's reluctance to discuss intimate matters of sex and marriage with her virgin daughter without the moral support of the Nurse suggests the strained relationship between mother and child, a relationship foiled by the warm, convivial rapport between Juliet and the earthy Nurse. Lord Capulet initially seems a fonder, more solicitous parent than his rather frigid wife, although he does not engage Juliet in onstage conversation until much later in the play, during a scene in which he violently rejects his daughter. A similar lack of communication typifies Romeo's relationship with his anxious father, who must seek out Romeo's friend Benvolio to inquire about Romeo's bizarre behavior. Romeo's failure ever to appear on stage with his parents highlights this alienation. . . . Not surprisingly, therefore, when the two adolescents, each an heir of the other's enemy clan, fall head over heels in love, they fail to confide their transcendent passions to their parents. Instead, the lovers marry secretly, embarking on a course that leads to catastrophe.

Although Romeo shares his self-indulgent infatuation for Rosaline with two friends, the skeptical Benvolio and the scoffing Mercutio, he is unwilling to divulge his rapturous love for Juliet to either of his comrades. Mercutio, part phallogocentric icon . . . part lord of misrule . . . equates love with sex and makes women the object of bawdy jeers; whereas romantic Romeo elevates women to a pedestal, macho Mercutio shoves them into the ditch. Marjorie Cox, employing the lexicon of Freudian psychoanalysis, explains Romeo and Mercutio as representing familiar antithetical responses to the sexual stresses occurring during adolescence. Romeo responds to the revival of libidinal energy by seeking an appropriate non-Oedipal love object to satisfy his desires, whereas Mercutio channels this upsurge of libido into mocking and avoiding women while seeking the exclusive company of his own sex (381–82, 385). The difference in psychological response erects a barrier that renders meaningful dialogue between the two friends virtually impossible. Understandably, therefore, Romeo hesitates to subject his ecstatic, private passion for Juliet to the ribald locker-room jests of his cynical sidekick Mercutio or even to the remonstrations of the more sympathetic but still skeptical Benvolio. However, Romeo's reluctance to confide in his friends proves fatal. . . .

Returning from his secret wedding to Juliet, Romeo encounters Benvolio, Mercutio, and Romeo's nemesis, Tybalt, in the sweltering town square, and impeded communication again serves as a catalyst to calamity. Furious that the scion of the enemy clan crashed the Capulet family's celebration and still smarting from Lord Capulet's stern rebuke, Tybalt has sent Romeo a written challenge, a missive obviously not received, because Romeo has not been home since the night of the ball. . . . Romeo, knowing nothing of Tybalt's challenge, hopes for reconciliation (had he known of the challenge, he might have been more cautious); Mercutio and Tybalt, knowing nothing of Romeo's private nuptials, misconstrue Romeo's attempts at peacemaking as cowardice. The result is a melee of misrecognition that leaves Mercutio and Tybalt dead and Romeo banished. The racking scene dramatizes the deleterious effect of masculine peer pressure on a sensitive adolescent, as Romeo allows his concern for masculine honor to overwhelm his love for Juliet and, unmanned by folly, kills his newly made cousin Tybalt. Escalus, the prince of Verona, arrives—as always, too late—and the state, which is unable throughout the play to maintain order, can only inflict punishment. The death of Tybalt unleashes the heretofore precariously restrained hostility between the two warring houses and combines with the demise of the far from "grave man," Mercutio, to signal the play's reversal from comedy to tragedy (3.1.97).[1] . . .

Commentators have traditionally interpreted Romeo and Juliet as either the *pharmakos* of Verona society or the victims of fate, chance, or even providence. Yet despite the monumentally bad luck suffered by the lovers, almost every circumstance leading to the tragedy can also be traced to an instance of impaired communication. Like the refrain of a poem linking stanza to stanza, the motif of occluded communication pervades the play, linking episode to episode. Had Romeo confided in Mercutio the details of his secret nuptials, his friend would certainly not have intervened in the altercation between Romeo and Tybalt. If either of the surrogate parents, the Friar or the Nurse, had possessed the nerve to confront the biological parents to confess their complicity in the concealed marriage, tragedy would doubtlessly have been averted. Had the eminently eligible Paris been told of Juliet's clandestine wedding, he would certainly not have pursued a married woman. Even the most salient example of fortune's animus, the quarantined messenger and the undelivered letter, results from failure to suit action to word and to provide necessary information. In a crucial epistle to Romeo, Friar Laurence outlines his harebrained scheme to give Juliet a potion that will simulate her death. This plan goes awry because Friar Laurence makes two major errors. First, he forgets his promise to entrust the letter to Romeo's servant Balthasar; and, second, he neglects to explain the importance of the missive to his surrogate messenger, Friar John. Thus Friar John meanders to a plague-ridden area in search of a companion for his journey, becomes quarantined, and never delivers the letter, whereas Balthasar, the expected messenger, rushes to Mantua with false information concerning Juliet's death. Through these many episodes of short-circuited communication, the play consistently reminds the audience that the calamitous deaths of five young people—Tybalt, Mercutio, Paris, Romeo, and Juliet—could all have been prevented had the citizens of Verona been able to talk candidly to one another. But the five youths and their bereaved parents, friends, and confidants all become victims of a conspiracy of silence.

The question has frequently been asked, Why do Romeo and Juliet commit suicide? . . .

Hostility toward both society and fortune, guilt over Tybalt's death, thwarted dreams and hope, and the loss of Juliet—all these contribute to Romeo's final hopelessness. Conversely, Juliet's self-murder lacks the anger, guilt, or even frustration characteristic of Romeo's last desperate hours. Rather, her suicide is rendered virtually inevitable by her progressive isolation resulting from the series of physical and psychological bereavements Juliet suffers in the last days of her life: the death of a cherished cousin; alienation from her father, mother, and nurse; desertion by the Friar; and, finally, the devastating loss of her beloved Romeo. Edwin Shneidman, a leading authority on suicide, insists that psychological pain, no matter how severe, "is endurable *if* the individual feels that he is truly not alone and can evoke some response in a significant other" (*Definition* 215; see also Farberow 391–92). But Juliet is ultimately stripped of all significant others, her total isolation symbolized by the hermetically sealed tomb in which, abandoned and alone, the adolescent girl takes her life.

Jerry Jacobs, in his analysis of adolescent suicide, follows Shneidman in speculating that persons commit suicide primarily because they encounter non-shareable problems. Jacobs further hypothesizes that adolescent suicide attempts result from "a chain reaction dissolution of any remaining meaningful social relationships in the days and weeks preceding the [suicide] attempt which leads to the adolescent's feeling that he has reached the 'end of hope'" (28). As I have tried to demonstrate, Shakespeare, that shrewd recorder of human behavior, anticipates in *Romeo and Juliet* the very factors identified by Jacobs and other prominent authorities on youth suicide . . . , factors that appear over and over again in clinical case studies on the subject: confused teenagers who seek to resolve conflicting psychosexual instincts; cold and authoritarian parents who impede the turbulent drives of adolescents toward individuation and fulfillment; impotent counselors; insensitive, often belligerent, peers; aggravating circumstances, particularly the loss of a loved one; frustration of primary needs; rage and defiance toward an environment perceived as hostile; helplessness and hopelessness; and, most agonizing of all, progressive isolation of the adolescents from meaningful social relationships. To a large degree, both in contemporary case studies of youth suicide and in *Romeo and Juliet*, this isolation results from the total severance of communication between the desperate teenagers and the narcissistic society that fails to heed their cry for help.

David Lucking remarks that not a single one of the written messages sent in the play arrives directly at its intended destination ("Balcony Scene" 6; see also Whittier 30–31n8). I further suggest that the letters that never arrive provide poignant emblems for the ubiquitous failed communication dramatized by the play—the spoken words that cannot be delivered, at least partially because the characters have quarantined their affections. . . . On the one hand, despite the blatant commodification of Juliet by her authoritarian parents, Capulet eloquently expresses his deep affection for Juliet (1.2.14–15), and both parents respond to their daughter's death with hyperbolic lamentations (4.5). Furthermore, although Romeo never appears in a domestic setting with his parents, his perplexed father seems genuinely concerned over his son's behavior, and Lady Montague dies of grief as a result of her son's banishment. On the other hand, the play clearly dramatizes a society plagued by alienation on all levels—the family, peer groups, the church, the state. Since the complex relation between Shakespeare's great love story and the society that produced it remains outside the purview of this essay, I will simply conclude by observing that the newspaper headlines daily assaulting and shocking even the most desensitized twentieth-century reader indicate that a similar alienation infects our contemporary society. No cure has yet been found for this dread disease, and this may be one of the reasons that, despite the gap of four hundred years, *Romeo and Juliet* speaks so urgently today to both young and old.

### Note
1. Citations to *Romeo and Juliet* in this essay are from *The Complete Works of Shakespeare*, edited by David Bevington.

## Arthur F. Kinney on Authority in *Romeo and Juliet*

The first disturbing moment in *Romeo and Juliet* comes in the opening lines of the Chorus, which struggles to be evenhanded and sure in its outline of a play about "A pair of star-crossed lovers":

> Two households, both alike in dignity,
>   In fair Verona, where we lay our scene,
> From ancient grudge break to new mutiny,
>   Where civil blood makes civil hands unclean.
> From forth the fatal loins of these two foes
>   A pair of star-crossed lovers take their life;
> Whose misadventured piteous overthrows
>   Doth with their death bury their parents' strife.
> The fearful passage of their death-marked love,
>   And the continuance of their parents' rage,
> Which, but their children's end, naught could remove,
>   Is now the two hours' traffic of our stage;
> The which if you with patient ears attend,
>   What here shall miss, our toil shall strive to mend. (prologue 1–14)[1] . . . .

Unlike the choruses that appear in other Shakespeare plays to set the scenes and set forth the issues, this one gives away the whole plot. Why . . . might Shakespeare reveal the plot? To remind a preoccupied audience of a familiar story? To provide a kind of program guide for the uninitiated? Or, more likely, to give the plot an interpretation that seems always already there? If the last is true, what is that interpretation? Can we break open the closed sonnet form of this speech that like Shakespeare's other sonnets describes a situation and then sums it up in a couplet that seems to close off the ideas with the form? Such phrases as "fatal loins," "star-crossed lovers," "fearful passage," "death-marked love," and even "continuance of their parents' rage," we note, tell us not only what will happen but also what we should think about dramatic events.

The deliberate parallel of "Two households" and "both alike in dignity" is echoed in "ancient grudge" and "new mutiny." Moreover, the phrases "civil blood" and "civil hands" (ends and means) seem to insist on balancing the past and the present that gives the opening of this play a static quality, a frozen sense of events that undermines narrative progression and dramatic development. Having read the chorus, why should we read the play? The most we can get out of the play is the how of the what, the details that, however we read and interpret them, we know will lead us to "death-marked love, / And the continuance of their parents' rage." The attempt of the younger generation to oppose their elders will wind up defeated, and the static situation in Verona will continue.

Not many . . . would settle for such a conclusion despite the preponderance of supporting evidence in these fourteen opening lines. So the search is on to prove me wrong, or at least to prove that Shakespeare is also doing something else. The something else . . . is in line 14: "What here shall miss." It is possible that the narrative summary here is incomplete, and so the judgments of the Chorus may be contingent. Rather than shut down the story of Romeo and Juliet, the Chorus opens it up. Yet if the Chorus, speaking on behalf of the actors, will by "toil . . . strive to mend" what is omitted from this twelve-line program note, does this suggest that what is omitted will only fill in the details of the outline already presented, interpreted, and, in a sense, evaluated? Or might the judgments, and therefore the narrative, of the Chorus itself be suspect—in need not so much of refinement as of alteration? We return one more time to the earlier lines, this time to look for too-easy generalizations, leaps in logic, or even inconsistencies. There is the uncertainty, for instance, of the undefined "ancient grudge" and, further, of how such a grudge could be an efficient cause for generations of strife. The past is hazy, the time span indefinite. Verona seems hardly "fair" in the picture the Chorus paints here; is there any reason for such a judgment to be sustained? Do the deaths of Romeo and Juliet "bury their parents' strife" as line 8 unequivocally states, or is there "continuance of their parents' rage" as line 10 unhesitatingly pronounces? It may be that these first fourteen lines are less pronouncement than rationalization, that the Chorus displays a troubling hope for change, a hope that is here posited only in Romeo and Juliet, "star-crossed lovers" whose "misadventure[s]" are nevertheless "piteous." . . .

The second chorus also bears examination:

> Now old desire doth in his deathbed lie,
>   And young affection gapes to be his heir;
> That fair for which love groaned for and would die,
>   With tender Juliet matched, is now not fair.
> Now Romeo is beloved and loves again,
>   Alike bewitched by the charm of looks;
> But to his foe supposed he must complain,
>   And she steal love's sweet bait from fearful hooks.
> Being held a foe, he may not have access
>   To breathe such vows as lovers use to swear,
> And she as much in love, her means much less
>   To meet her new beloved anywhere;
> But passion lends them power, time means, to meet,
> Temp'ring extremities with extreme sweet. (1–14)

The question is, has anything changed? The form of this chorus is identical to that of the first—the closed Shakespearean sonnet, in which three quatrains are brought to completion by a rhymed couplet. But the whole substance has changed, from plot to process. The time scheme has changed, from the vast and distant overview to the involvement of in medias res: "Now." Judgments in the lines are open to question: "That fair . . . is now not fair." "[L]ove's sweet bait" is associated with "fearful hooks," and the implication is that Juliet should be aware of this, as should Romeo. What appears one-dimensional in the first chorus now seems rife with disturbing paradoxes. . . . In "Temp'ring extremities with extreme sweet" statements have now become propositions. The Chorus arguably stops speaking because it has run out of information and is waiting until more actions unfold. The Chorus has been transformed, perhaps by the power of passion, from program note to playhouse spectator and auditor. The Chorus is no longer telling us but rather mediating for us and becoming like us. We join forces with the Chorus to mediate (that is, interpret and anticipate).

The next question . . . is . . . if the Chorus moves from telling us to guiding us, what does it do next? The answer is that it disappears—a disappearance as startling as that in *The Taming of a Shrew* of Christopher Sly. Why . . . would Shakespeare dismiss the Chorus?

The answer . . . is that the role of the Chorus is subsumed by other characters in the play. Since that role is one of authority, a suitable candidate appears only three scenes later when Friar Lawrence, in the soliloquy at his first appearance, adopts the same knowing, oracular role the Chorus had. . . .

But a closer look at Friar Lawrence, even in his opening speech, also raises questions about knowledge and self-knowledge. "Within the infant rind of this weak flower," he notes, "Poison hath residence and medicine power" (23–24). He concludes:

> Two such opposed kings encamp them still
> In man as well as herbs—grace and rude will;
> And where the worser is predominant,
> Full soon the canker death eats up that plant. (27–30)

The Friar's sense of paradox here, however, is no greater than that of the maturing Juliet, who has just told Romeo that "I should kill thee with much cherishing" (2.2.183) if given the chance. The Friar, moreover, seems confused, for in claiming to exercise grace in dealing with the young lovers he in fact imposes his own rude will without hesitation or modesty. What begins in 2.3 as a chastisement of Romeo for his swift dismissal of Rosaline for Juliet only anticipates the swift way in which the Friar takes upon himself the task of ending the generations-old feud. He does not at first attempt to enter the civil realm of Prince Escalus, whose division of Verona by separating the Capulets from the Montagues only prolongs the feud (1.1.84–106), but in fact he usurps that realm by attempting singlehandedly to end the ancient grudge himself:

But come, young waverer, come go with me.
In one respect I'll thy assistant be;
For this alliance may so happy prove
To turn your households' rancor to pure love. (2.3.89–92)

Having stressed to himself (and to Romeo) the paradoxes in nature, the Friar now forgets all possibilities of paradox when, paradoxically, he volunteers for the duty of the Prince. But this unholy matrimony of church and state—which dissolves in the play's final scene, when the Friar inversely confesses to the Prince and the Prince absolves him—is not the worst of the Friar's disregard for the law. Hearing the confessions of Romeo and Juliet as might a priest (but not a friar), Friar Lawrence marries them secretly, without the traditional banns, thus violating the sacrament of his church.

This act itself hangs on a nice paradox. . . . On the one hand, Catholic practices may be sacrificed here—the Elizabethan Shakespeare, writing for a Protestant England after the Reformation, sets evil practices in Catholic Verona. But, on the other hand, in Elizabethan England an alternative to the practice of pronouncing banns three times before the church service of matrimony was the practice known as *sponsalia de praesenti*, whereby vows were exchanged in the presence of a witness (and what better witness to such a pledge than a man of the church?). The vows, though subject to consecration at a later time, were held to constitute full marriage. The problem, of course, is that this premarital contract—on which the action of *Measure for Measure* also turns—is a Protestant ritual, not a Catholic one. . . . However we leave this discussion—which may be impossible to resolve fully, since knowledge in this play is always potentially paradoxical rather than parabolic—we note that in due course the Friar will attempt to master life and death by helping Romeo to a secret exile and by giving Juliet a potion that (as she makes clear in her soliloquy in 4.3) may literally be a matter of life and death. The Friar would not only be priest but also Prince and God.

Who then *has* the necessary authority in this play? Not the elder Montagues, for all their concern for their son, or the Capulets, for all their disregard for the opinions and desires of their daughter. Like the Friar, the two families are limited—the Montagues by hoping for a rosier world in the future, the Capulets by using force to achieve their way. Not the Nurse, whose earthiness is finally both too worldly and too banal. Not Benvolio, whose optimistic attitude, like that of Romeo's father, knows little doubt and naively concentrates on wishing Romeo well. Not in Mercutio, for all his wisdom about the dangers of dreaming (a pointed lesson for Romeo); when driven to accidental death, he would set an epidemic free indiscriminately: "A plague a'both your houses! . . . Your houses!" (3.1.108–10; cf. 92). Mercutio's condemnation is at best a throwback to the equivocation of the first Chorus. Not in Tybalt initially or in Paris finally, the latter of whom would forsake justice and mercy for vengeance.

Instead, authority rests—if it rests anywhere—in the tragic heroes themselves. Juliet's choice and dismissal of aid from her parents, then her confessor, and finally her nurse show that Juliet is driven back to her own best judgments as, holding the vial in her hands, she measures the consequences of a potion that may work or may fail. In each instance, she chooses constantly. (Seen in this light, the Chorus's insistence that she is "star-crossed" is woefully misguided.) Sequentially, but in a kind of parallel, Romeo's choice to face death by returning at once to Verona is embodied in his decision to pause in Mantua to visit an apothecary and choose, literally, his own poison. Here, as later in the tomb, he will, like Juliet, voluntarily choose death. They die by no authority but their own; if they take on themselves the sins of their fathers (their *births* were "star-crossed"), they also take on themselves responsibility for their choice to marry secretly in the Friar's cell. . . .

The need for the lovers to die in this play is not entirely of their own choosing, . . . because Romeo and Juliet were born into an ancient grudge not of their making. But the characters' sense of responsibility seems central to the final actions of the play when the Friar, returning to his function as chorus, gives a synopsis of the play and offers himself as a sacrifice (5.3.267–68), seeming to know that his special role will save him. So it does, and when the Prince says, "We still have known thee for a holy man" (270), he excuses both the Friar and himself. . . . The Prince excuses the Friar—lets him off without any civil punishment—because the Friar is "a holy man" and therefore, apparently, answerable to a different, higher authority. But the line also betrays the Prince, who surrendered his authority early in the play by failing to provide justice and prevent bloodshed. Finally, the two sets of parents vie in establishing memorials for the deceased lovers, beginning a variant of the feud all over again. The Prince's final pronouncement of "A glooming peace" (5.3.305) openly subscribes to this failure.

In stark contrast to their elders, the young lovers, lying dead, have made choices and exercised responsibility and punishment. If Romeo and Juliet's sense of justice (and love) does not teach any of those who remain on stage, their bodies lie there as silent emblems of authority and responsibility. If we attempt to stage this last scene in our minds . . . we see that the characters crowd on the stage as they have in only two other scenes in the play: the masked ball and the fight between the Capulets and the Montagues in 1.1. (The latter scene contrasts with the fight in 3.2 where the chief Montague refuses to engage in combat.) In fact, Romeo does not fight in the first scene either (he is absent) and Juliet is in neither scene. Now that Romeo and Juliet appear with all the others for the first time, their silent presence judges everyone else.

There is another way to look at the staging scenes in the play. Given a discovery space that might hold large props or suggest privacy, the three episodes necessarily at the rear of the stage, taking up the same theatrical space, are the bedroom scenes and the scenes in the Friar's cell (and the apothecary shop), and all are displaced by the large tombs at the end. The bedroom tempts the body, the cell tempts the soul, but both temptations are overcome in the graveyard when the lovers voluntarily reunite. In the end, the dead teach us, the living; Romeo and Juliet, through their actions, experiences, and choices, finally meld paradox and parable. But they do more— by embodying the tragic significance of their story, they make the play's final choric comment. They displace the earlier, more limited Chorus because their wider, deeper comment on the risk and cost of life is one that the Chorus never understood. The authority of Romeo and Juliet . . . is the authority the play has been searching for.

### Note

1. Citations to *Romeo and Juliet* in this essay are from the J. A. Bryant, Jr., edition.

## STEPHEN M. BUHLER ON *ROMEO AND JULIET*, MEDIA "REPACKAGING," *WEST SIDE STORY*, AND BRUCE SPRINGSTEEN

Romeo and Juliet are ubiquitous figures in popular and mass-market culture and have been for well over a century, perhaps for as long as marketing strategies have appropriated from works increasingly set as "high culture." Over the course of that century, references to "Juliet and her Romeo" (5.3.310)[1]—as the Prince names the couple and characterizes their story in his concluding couplet—changed as the play became more strongly identified with youth and with shifting societal attitudes toward the young. Adolescence, the period of development called to mind by the characters' chronological ages, came to be seen as a subculture with its own behavior patterns, tastes, and purchasing power. Many of this group's attributes were constructed and communicated in and through music.

In this essay, I will focus on how Romeo and Juliet have been depicted and transformed in mass-marketed pop music directed primarily at young audiences and, secondarily, at audiences who have identified themselves with youth culture. The characters' representation in "post-pop" music, much of which borrows from pop music idioms but deliberately distances itself from mass-market strategies, built—and continue to build—on earlier transformations. Such repackaging was not an isolated series of encounters between literature and the marketplace: it was part of a larger dynamic of exchange between competing and complementary sources of culture. The U.S. educational system, as well as the music industry, configured adolescents as an audience to be reached—as, in effect, consumers. What resulted in connection with *Romeo and Juliet* was a widespread reconsideration of the play's significance and of its leading characters. Marketing did not determine, but instead encouraged new interpretations. As my title suggests, the repackaging led to markedly different understandings of who Romeo and Juliet could be, of the qualities and behaviors with which they could instantly be associated. Romeo, at one time the embodiment of suave insincerity, was recast as passionate commitment personified; Juliet, formerly presented as merely reactive to her lover's blandishments, has shown signs of increased independence and agency. Many of these shifts in characterization have gained force not only by virtue of the music that drives the songs or of the societal attitudes that provide their context: they also gain force by virtue of engagements with the playtexts (and *Romeo and Juliet* has a vexed textual history[2]) that are the songs' direct and indirect inspiration. Perhaps most curiously and productively of all, economic factors that contributed to the transformations have also appeared overtly in song lyrics reflecting and shaping popular understandings of these two characters. . . .

The marketplace serves as a reminder that Romeo and Juliet are not stable, set personalities in the playtexts that have been brought back to life, thanks to pop music. Nevertheless, the characters and the playtexts from which they emerge have been seen as more lively, more vital after being reworked in pop musical culture: in this sense, they have been revived. Romeo as a young person is taken more seriously when young people take themselves more seriously and are encouraged to do so by the cultural productions in which they participate as consumers, audiences, and (at times) producers. He cannot be readily dismissed when his sincerity is not so easily questioned. Juliet, too, provides a mirror of social attitudes toward adolescent females. In this, she is similar to Ophelia, whose name has appeared—with but a single paragraph of justification (Pipher 20)—in the title of *Reviving Ophelia*, a bestselling book devoted to "Saving the Selves of Adolescent Girls." Over the centuries, the character of Juliet has been rewritten in accordance with shifting notions of identity and propriety for very young women. Sometimes the language has been gutted, removing "all sexual innuendo and other subtleties from her speech, transforming her into a perfectly innocent heroine" acceptable to audiences of a given era (Levenson 22). Sometimes her age has been quietly adjusted upward, making the inclusion of such complexities less distasteful. Certainly critical views that stress the "purity" and "innocence" of Shakespeare's protagonists and their love participate in similarly mirroring processes. Representations of Juliet that acknowledge her agency in several spheres of action appeal (in both senses of the term) to shifting notions and self-images of girlhood and young womanhood. . . .

Pop music depictions of Juliet's character from the early 1960s on are often influenced by *West Side Story*. This Broadway musical adaptation of *Romeo and Juliet* debuted in 1957 with a book by Arthur Laurents, lyrics by Stephen Sondheim, and music by Leonard Bernstein. The impact of the musical intensified after the highly successful 1961 United Artists release of a film version, which received industry acclaim (including ten Academy Awards) along with critical and audience approval. *West Side Story* participates in the larger cultural trend linking the situations in Shakespeare's play with the circumstances faced by contemporary U.S. youth, but presciently marks youth as self-consciously marginalized and resistant. Adult society fades into the background in this version; its role in establishing and sustaining the deadly feud, so evident in the playtexts, is almost thoroughly suppressed. Flaming youth is personified here in the "juvenile delinquent" members of rival, ethnically-based gangs and even the surrogate father-figure of Friar Laurence is largely subsumed by a dress-maker's mannequin, which "officiates" at the exchange of vows between Tony and Maria. The importance of *West Side Story* in reinforcing views of these characters can be seen in Franco Zeffirelli's 1968 film version, which featured a daringly youthful cast and offered a distinctive "generation gap" reading of the play. As Kenneth Rothwell has observed, *Romeo and Juliet* "has always been a tale *about* but not necessarily *for* young people" and Zeffirelli, encouraged by Bernstein's musical and current trends of thought, made a film that was deeply connected to youth culture and therefore "palatable" to younger audiences (Rothwell 134–35). It proved so palatable that Nino Roti's music spawned several pop music hits: his song for the film, "What Is A Youth?," draws additional attention to generational factors while cleverly invoking Renaissance variations on the *carpe diem* theme; with new lyrics—and also as an instrumental—it appeared as "A Time for Us" and was widely covered by a range of artists. The new lyrics draw upon one of Bernstein's and Sondheim's most celebrated songs from *West Side Story*, "Somewhere," which begins "There's a place for us" and includes, in the next verse, "There's a time for us." The borrowing makes the musical's influence on Zeffirelli's film and on the film's reception still more obvious.

The pop songwriter who has, arguably, been the most haunted by these specific representations of *Romeo and Juliet* and similar reworkings of Shakespeare's characters is Bruce Springsteen, who rings provocative changes on the story and specifically on the depiction of Juliet. The romanticized view of adolescent street life that Bernstein, Laurents, and Sondheim helped to perpetuate in *West Side Story* also provides a more general framework for Springsteen, whose depictions of Atlantic Seaboard urban life aspire to lush tragedy or mythic resonance. Springsteen makes direct allusions to both Romeo and Juliet in at least three very different songs: "Incident on 57th Street," on his second album, *The Wild, the Innocent, and the E Street Shuffle* (1973); "Fire," recorded by the Pointer Sisters in 1979 and frequently performed by Springsteen himself in concert; and "Point Blank," on the 1980 album *The River*. All three songs suggest a Juliet that can choose not to participate in the tragic sequence of events and therefore reflect a Juliet that is an instrumental figure, rather than complementary one, in Shakespeare's rendering of the tale.

"Incident on 57th Street" presents its protagonist and the object of his desire in Shakespearean terms, as filtered through

*West Side Story.* "Spanish Johnny" is distinguished from his peers ("Those romantic young boys, all they ever want to do is fight") by his love for "Puerto Rican Jane," who shares her ethnic identity with the Broadway musical's Sharks and with Maria, its Juliet figure:

> Well, like a cool Romeo, he made his moves;
> Oh, she looked so fine.
> Like a late Juliet, she knew he'd never be true,
> But then she really didn't mind.
> Upstairs a band was playin',
> The singer was singin' something about goin' home.
> She whispered, "Spanish Johnny, you can leave me tonight,
> But just don't leave me alone."

Unlike earlier songs that had found Shakespeare's characters possibly lacking in passion or commitment, "Incident on 57th Street" suggests that its own characters are aware both of their tragic precedents and of their inability or refusal to imitate them. Johnny, partly following Romeo's example, is inspired by his lady's beauty to act. He remains "cool," however, following the advice of Sondheim's Jets to be so ("Just play it cool, boy, real cool") and limited by his own era's conventions. Johnny apparently feels that he cannot directly invoke the extravagant expressions of desire that were available to Shakespeare's Romeo and that were open to Juliet's initial skepticism. The lateness of the late-twentieth century Juliet is also connected to a kind of coolness: she will not hurry into either a statement of trust or one of devotion. Shakespeare's Juliet, though mindful that the newfound love is "too rash, too unadvis'd, too sudden" (2.2.118), will still only delay until the exchange of solemn vows the very next day. Johnny's would-be lady love is no fool, neither rushing into things nor promising more than she cares to deliver. Despite the awareness of the difference, there is no direct confession of regret, although the "really didn't mind" can register as ironic and rueful, given the expression of need that follows.

The original speaker in "Fire" can come across as more of a "roaming Romeo" than the devoted variety, a throwback to the sophisticated vision of the character that dominated pop culture references before the advent of youth subculture. Springsteen's persona here has a number of come-on lines that expertly reject the lady's repeated refusals: this version of Puerto Rican Jane cannot have the last word. Once again, however, a change in the gender of the singer and of the implied speaker can deeply affect how the lyrics register on the listener. In the Pointer Sisters' presentation, the lady herself admits that her statements of rejection are false: "My words say, 'split!' But my words, they lie." The suggestion of duplicity becomes explicit in the lines,

> Romeo and Juliet, Samson and Delilah,
> Baby, you can bet their love they didn't deny.

The juxtapositioning of those two couples is striking. A male speaker may be obliquely asserting that if anyone has to be worried in this case, it's himself: why should she be reluctant when he has, supposedly, more to lose? A female speaker, in contrast, may be giving her addressee fair warning: don't presume on either her responsiveness or his security. In both cases, it isn't clear (as seen in "Fever") whether the couples are meant to be thought of as contrasts or complements. Juliet may be presented as Delilah's opposite; after all, Juliet goes against "her people" even as Delilah chooses to remain loyal to the Philistine tribe. But the lyrics also group all four lovers together, since none of them denied their initial attraction. Should Juliet be seen as a Delilah-figure, someone responsible for the downfall of her beloved?

The Pointer Sisters' playful eroticism (nearly growling the first syllable of Romeo's name) in performance matches the songwriter's lighter touch in the song. Springsteen's ambivalence toward Juliet comes across far more sharply in "Point Blank." Much of *The River*, the album on which the song appears, is devoted to disappointments and disillusionments, to what happens when youthful idealism is confronted with hard, especially economic reality. In this song, both Springsteen and his speaker draw contrasts between a present situation and two different renderings of the story of *Romeo and Juliet*:

I was gonna be your Romeo
You were gonna be my Juliet
These days you don't wait for Romeos
You wait on that welfare check
And on all the pretty things that you can't ever have.

Springsteen here draws upon the consumerist heart of the Reflections' "(Just Like) Romeo and Juliet," as well as the precedent of the source play. He also expands upon the logic of a passive female protagonist, as assumed in the earlier song: this Juliet cannot take action, but can only wait for one form of rescue or another. She chooses to wait for basic subsistence and for (perhaps) the products held out as a promise to participants in the U.S. economic system; she, too, cannot wait for alternative and questionable values. Springsteen suggests, however, that this is a conscious choice: all Juliets, now, can be credited or blamed with some measure of autonomy.

### Note
1. All citations from Shakespeare's plays are taken from *The Riverside Shakespeare*, second edition.
2. Reconsiderations of the varying texts' value are offered by Halio and Urkowitz.

## PETER S. DONALDSON OFFERS SOME THOUGHTS ON BAZ LUHRMANN'S *ROMEO + JULIET*

In a sense the story of Romeo and Juliet has always had two endings, one tending to sentimental melodrama and the other toward the bleak acknowledgments of the tragic mode. David Garrick was said to have performed a "happy" ending in which the lovers survive, alternating this version on successive nights with Shakespeare's bleaker conclusion. Even in Shakespeare, where the lovers die in both the First Quarto and in the Second Quarto/Folio version, which is the basis of the modern edition, there are differences. In neither are the lovers conscious at the same moment, but Q1 suggest, far more strongly than Q2/F that there will be a meeting after death. In the received text, Juliet's final lines are "Unhappy dagger / This is thy sheath; there rust and let me die," while the First Quarto suggests a reunion like that of Antony and Cleopatra: "this shall end my fear / Rest in my bosom, thus I come to thee."

Luhrmann's version embodies the doubleness of the tradition. His media allegory concludes as a cruel triumph of the spectacle, with an astonishingly deliberate and poignant gunshot, all too familiar-looking footage of urban news coverage of the event, with the ubiquitous television screen having the last word. But within that framing, the death scene *also* honors the promptings of the text and the tradition toward a more redeeming and transcending conclusion, and I believe does so in a way that affects what the film has to say about the relation of contemporary media to the arts and media of the past.

First—the "Church of the Traffic Warden" is not only the most icon-saturated space in the film. It is also a space that we quickly come to see as a dignified, beautiful, ennobling setting for tragedy; perhaps, in the process, adjusting prejudices against visual excess the film itself has endorsed and deployed in its use of "Latin" religiosity as critique of commodified religion. At the beginning of the sequence, the saturation of the thousand and more candles, interspersed with large neon crosses threatens to overwhelm the human meaning of anything that might happen in it—there is no sanctuary, no space apart, no place not filled with the "brand names" of "Dark Ages." Yet as the sequence proceeds the harmony of this aesthetic may be distinguished from the jarring juxtapositions of mass-produced Christian images and breezy violence we have seen earlier, and this "techno-Baroque" interior joins with other elements in the staging and soundtrack to move, very firmly, toward the sacred and away from wit, satire, or critique. As Romeo first peers into the church, then enters it, walks down its aisle to the place of the altar where Juliet's body lies, we recognize this as the place where Romeo and Juliet were married; as shots proceed from wide shots to close-ups of Romeo, the myriad candles shift function, from markers of excess to resonance with his grief, and then, as we draw nearer still, to light sources, tender, appropriate, and, as life and death alternate as presences within the sequence, as images of a poignant transience.

If one image of the "end" of *William Shakespeare's Romeo + Juliet* is of body bags on gurneys moving into separate ambulances, another is the striking illusion that follows Juliet's death, created by filming the lovers with moving cameras hoisted on ropes and pulleys, in which Romeo and Juliet, embracing on the bier on which they die, seem to float above us in apotheosis, like the figures in a *trompe l'oeil* ceiling, while the *liebestod* from *Tristan and Isolde* plays on the soundtrack. This ending is closer to the hints of transcendental closure suggested by the First Quarto's "rest in my bosom / Thus I come to thee" and effects a final and powerful recuperation of the religious motifs in the film. Barbara Hodgdon (1999) has recently argued that the "double ending" mirrors both the realities of modern urban life that young people face as well as the continued vitality (and necessity) of romance traditions in contemporary youth culture.

In doing so, the sequence also continues and concludes the film's association of the alternative world the lovers hoped to create with the arts and media of the past. Traces and reminders of that world have been present in the film all along—in Mercutio's performances, in the dominating image of the ruined theater, and pervasively in the many ways in which the film's citations and surrogations make us aware that the film is not classical or authorized Shakespeare even as they reiterate and refresh the traditional construction of Shakespeare's *Romeo and Juliet* as a paradigm of romantic love. Now, in the final sequences shot in the cathedral, allusions to the past predominate, reaching beyond Shakespeare to include Medieval romance, Wagnerian opera, and Baroque illusionist painting, all invoked to reinforce the association of traditional art forms and legacy media with romantic love. Most important, such "citations" are no longer comic or ironic, but now blend seamlessly with the contemporary, slow-paced romantic style associated with the lovers and first seen in the film when Romeo is introduced writing Petrarchan poetry.

The convergence of Luhrmann's romantic style with an unironic use of Richard Wagner and Tiepolo may blunt the film's edge as media critique and call in question aspects of my argument, which has invited the reader to notice ways in which the film carries on radical traditions of ideological demystification, from Feuerbach and Marx through Guy Debord, punk, Gothic, and gay activist subcultures and styles. If Luhrmann's film is convergent with the aesthetic strategies and resignifications of the Sydney Gay and Lesbian Mardi Gras, it is also open to the valid criticism, urged even by the founders and original participants in the Mardi Gras, that the event has been co-opted, transformed by its success into a celebration of mainstream culture (Searle 1998; Jones 1997). But, understood differently, Luhrmann's double ending may deepen its value as critique. Following the rich ambivalences and oscillations of Shakespeare's ending, Luhrmann's *Romeo + Juliet* attempts to give its allegory of life in the age of media spectacle the stature of tragedy.

## LESLIE BRODER ON HEROISM AGAINST THE ODDS IN THE PLAY

In *Romeo and Juliet*, a broiling Verona summer provides a volatile backdrop for Romeo and Juliet's passion and their families' rancor. Although male aggression fuels the play, Juliet blossoms as a sturdy, intelligent woman whose devotion to her love and her ideals makes her heroic.

The feud between the families is continually described in terms of misogynistic violence. When the Capulets' servingmen discuss how they would fight the Montagues, Sampson declares, "women, being the / weaker vessels, are ever thrust to the wall. Therefore / I will push Montague's men from the wall and thrust his maids to the wall" (9). Here, showing power over enemies is equivalent to sexually mauling women. That this conversation occurs in the opening scene highlights the centrality of masculine power and feminine submission against which Juliet must fight.

Capulet plays the dominant role society has set for him when he shows his aggression toward and power over daughter Juliet. He hesitates when Paris wants to marry her, for mothers "too soon marred are those so early made" (27). Although it was customary for upper-class children to marry at a young age to preserve their families' wealth, he senses thirteen is too young for his daughter to wed. Nevertheless, he reverts to brutality when Juliet refuses to marry Paris. He curses, "Out, you green-sickness carrion! Out, you baggage! / . . . I tell thee what: get thee to church o' Thursday, / Or never after look me in the face" (167). Her disobedience to his will is an egregious and unacceptable affront. Whether or not Capulet even considers her best interests, finally, he makes his decision about Juliet's marriage partner to satisfy his own needs, not her desires.

Unlike Juliet, who resists easy stereotyping and patriarchal domination, the Nurse obeys male authority. After Romeo's banishment, the Nurse advises Juliet to marry Paris for, "Romeo's a dishclout to him. . . . / Your first is dead, or 'twere as good he were" (171–73). The Nurse believes it is better that Juliet meekly marry someone she does not love than take the risk of meeting secretly with Romeo. Lady Capulet, too, submits to a man's will, as she is the agent for her husband's wishes. She broaches the subject of marriage with Juliet, scolds her when she mourns Tybalt's death too long, and swears, "Do as thou wilt, for I have done with thee" when she refuses to wed Paris (171). Besides the tears she sheds at Juliet's death, Lady Capulet only interacts with her daughter to transmit her husband's thoughts.

Although men are ostensibly the dominant power, Juliet often shows greater sense and strength of character than does Romeo. While Romeo is given to pining for his love with extravagant phrases, Juliet restrains him when he goes too far. She chastises him when he swears his love by the moon, "O, swear not by the moon, th' inconstant moon, / That monthly changes in her [circled] orb, / Lest that thy love prove likewise variable" (77). During this exchange, Juliet takes decisive action to consummate their love through marriage. She is also more reasonable when facing adversity. After Romeo is banished for killing Tybalt, he is insensible. He cannot stop weeping and threatens to stab himself. Friar Lawrence insults him by calling him feminine. "Art thou a man? Thy form cries out thou art. / Thy tears are womanish . . ." (149). While the Friar sees only a man disgracing himself, Juliet is better able to reason, despite her grief: "That villain cousin would have killed my husband. / Back, foolish tears, back to your native spring" (137).

Students should be alerted to Juliet's courage; it may be difficult for them to understand how radical she is for her time. In a patriarchal culture where women are men's subjects, she stands against her father's wishes to marry Paris without hesitation. Juliet remains true to her conscience and inner desires. She begs Friar Lawrence, "O, bid me leap, rather than marry Paris, / From off the battlements of any tower, / . . . And I will do it without fear or doubt" (183). She then acts on her words by drinking the sleeping drought, seeking comfort from neither her Nurse nor her mother. When she wakes in the tomb to find Friar Lawrence panicking and Romeo dead, she doesn't flee for safety with the Friar. As he departs in fear, she faces eternity and death alone. Her final deed is to violently stab herself without flinching. Throughout these trying scenes, Juliet debunks her society's notion that a woman is weak, inconstant, and incapable of bravery.

Although she commits the desperate act of suicide, Juliet can still be a model of certain strengths, helpful for young people to observe. Amidst a reckless feud, she displays morality, fortitude, and wit. . . .

Juliet embodies a marvelous melding of innocence and foresight. Her innocence is clear as she is enraptured in the ecstasy of her first love; at the same time, she is perceptive enough to envision its brutal end. As her family engages in a fierce battle, charged by masculine antagonism, she remains resolute and heroic. Her strength must come from within, for her father seeks to dominate women and her mother accepts his right to do so. The question remains, then, why Juliet decides to commit suicide when her bravery should allow her to face her family or flee Verona; students should consider whether these, or other options, were viable in her time.

**Work Cited**

Shakespeare, William. *Romeo and Juliet* [ca. 1599]. Ed. Barbara A. Mowat and Paul Werstine. New York: Washington Square-Pocket, 1992.

## JAY L. HALIO ON "AUTHENTIC" VERSUS "LIVING" SHAKESPEARE

Of what use is it today to know how *Romeo and Juliet* was staged in previous centuries? Well, for one thing, it shows that actors, directors, producers are constantly trying to render Shakespeare's plays in ways that speak directly to their audiences. In the nineteenth century, producers understood the interest of their age in historical accuracy, at least as regards the stage settings of the plays; they therefore went to considerable lengths to reproduce Verona as they thought, after serious scholarly investigation, Verona must have looked in the sixteenth century. This was no concern in Shakespeare's day or in the seventeenth or eighteenth centuries, when the actors dressed in the fashion of their own times. Today, we sometimes see modern dress productions and productions in Elizabethan settings. Which is preferable? And what happens when Shakespeare's play is transformed to another medium—opera, ballet, or film?

Let's take the first question first: modern dress or Elizabethan setting.[16] In 1986 the Royal Shakespeare Company performed *Romeo and Juliet* in present-day Verona, complete with swimming pool, camcorders (for the final scene, staged as a media event), and even an Alfa-Romeo sports car driven onto the set. Michael Bogdanov directed and, as he always does, insisted on bringing Shakespeare up to date. Hence the cast resembled many contemporary types: teenage gang members, Italian business tycoons, socially ambitious wives, bored young men and women straight out of *La Dolce Vita*. Of course, in transposing time frames, Bogdanov had to make certain adjustments: switchblade knives replaced rapiers, and Romeo killed himself with an overdose of drugs administered by a hypodermic needle. These are incidentals, after all.[17] Although the script was cut ... the dialogue was not otherwise seriously altered, and no funeral procession was added, although golden statues of Romeo and Juliet were on view during the concluding media event.[18]

That is the point, the main one, it seems to me—preserving as much as possible of Shakespeare's language. Not all of it is essential, as the 1597 quarto (Q1) demonstrates. We need not genuflect, as some pedants do, before Shakespeare's oeuvre and insist on preserving every last word in performance.[19] Shakespeare knew that some passages might prove expendable, and producers through the centuries have known it. . . . But "translating" Shakespeare into modern verse, or worse, is something else again. No one would defend these days what Garrick did to *Romeon and Juliet* in act 5, when he had Romeo and Juliet engage in dialogue after Romeo swallowed his fatal draught. True, when deletions of the script are made, some bridging of the text needs to be done, and a careful splice becomes necessary. . . .

Key to Shakespearean performance, whether it is *Romeo and Juliet* or some other play, is not the setting, which should probably be kept as simple as possible to avoid the excesses of "designer theater" (Ralph Berry's term). No, the key is interpretation, and here is where shaping the playscript can exercise a decided if sometimes subtle influence, as Charlotte Cushman's script showed. How important are Mercutio and the nurse? By reducing their roles, eighteenth- and nineteenth-century producers distorted Shakespeare's original, removing from it much of the earthy aspect of human love that contrasts with Romeo and Juliet's experience but is also a part of it. Again, what happens when, as Garrick did, you eliminate references to Rosaline and omit or muzzle Romeo's Petrarchan love lines? An important dimension of the play gets lost. But is every line that Friar Lawrence speaks necessary? Can't his lengthier speeches be shortened without similar distortions? I think they can, and so do many directors, past and present, who curtail the worthy friar's verbosity. Again, does every conceit in Romeo's or Juliet's love lyrics have to be preserved, or can a staging of the play dispense with some, though not all, of them?

These are the kinds of questions that staging *Romeo and Juliet*—and many other plays—involves. But prior to all of them is the vexed issue of directorial concept. At what point does the overall interpretation of the play—the one that helps determine the size and shape of the playscript but also the interpretation of roles, the set design, stage business, and much else—come into being? Some directors fix their concepts before their actors are even cast; in fact, the concept may determine who will play what role. In 1960 Franco Zeffirelli, directing the play for the Old Vic in London, determined from the outset to emphasize the play as a young person's tragedy, which of course it is; therefore, he used young actors for his principal leads, casting John Strike and Judi Dench as the young lovers. It was a good choice, though when it came to his film version, Olivia Hussey and Leonard Whiting did not have the training or the experience that such roles require, and spectacle more than acting dominated the production—inevitably, perhaps, given the medium of film. Recently, a production in Israel used a multiethnic cast to highlight contemporary conflicts—Israelis versus Arabs as Montagues and Capulets.[20] Similarly, in January 1999 a student production at the University of Virginia, concerned with racism on and off campus, cast white actors as Montagues and black actors as Capulets.[21] Are such transpositions not only of time and place but of ethnicity legitimate? While on the one hand they tend to localize the conflicts inherent in the play, on the other they also universalize them as they make them more specific; indeed, by making them specific they encourage universalization.[22]

A production's scenography is only one way of addressing—or dressing up—the play's Shakespearean "meanings," and not the most important. Modern dress settings are ultimately a superficial means of coming to grips with a play in an attempt to "make it new." If we believe with Ben Jonson that Shakespeare's plays were not of an age but for all time, then "making it new" really means revitalizing our experience in such a way that we see and feel and understand Shakespeare's plays as contemporary artifacts speaking directly to us. . . .

What I have been arguing throughout this paper, using *Romeo and Juliet* as an example, is for the reconsideration of the concept of authenticity as a criterion for Shakespearean performance. In his important book, *Shakespeare and the*

*Authority of Performance*, William Worthen has aptly discussed the issue, and much of my argument (as my references indicate) relies upon some of those he puts forward, though more eloquently and at greater length. At the risk of oversimplifying his position, let me agree that the authenticity, or "authority," of a performance is by no means so closely identified as it may seem with the printed texts of Shakespeare's plays, which themselves involve questions of authenticity. . . . Increasingly today, thanks to the growing abundance of performance criticism, which includes detailed reviews of Shakespearean productions such as *Shakespeare Bulletin* publishes several times a year, the tradition of performance has begun to reassert itself among scholars. This is decidedly not to say that editions, as "authentic" as modern scholars can make them, are irrelevant to the appraisal of Shakespeare's plays in performance. Shakespeare's language is still primary. But it is not the single or sole reference point for understanding "Shakespeare." It is where we begin, necessarily, and it is where we must return when productions of his plays are concerned. Literary analysis and theatrical analysis have, or should have, a symbiotic relation to each other. In the best scholarship and criticism, as in the best performances, they always do.

### Notes

16. Shakespeare's comedies seem to lend themselves to modern settings more easily than his tragedies or histories: see Berry, Ralph. 1989. *On Directing Shakespeare*. London: Hamish Hamilton, 14–16. If this is true, I am not sure why, although Berry suggests it may be because the stakes for fidelity to Shakespeare's original may be higher. *Romeo and Juliet* violates this rule (if it is a rule), possibly because the first half is so comic. Not until Mercutio's death and Romeo's revenge against Tybalt does the play pivot around to tragedy.

17. Compare Worthen 1997, 141: "Putting Shakespeare on the modern stage may give us insight into our condition, but it doesn't change Shakespeare—it just dresses him in new clothes."

18. See Kennedy, Dennis. 1993. *Looking at Shakespeare*. Cambridge: Cambridge University Press, 297–300. Kennedy notes that at the end the prince spoke the first eight lines of the prologue instead of the familiar concluding lines of the play. He compares this curtailed ending with Henry Irving's a hundred years earlier. See also Clayton, Thomas. 1989. "'Balancing at Work': (R)evoking the Script in

Performance and Criticism." *Shakespeare and the Sense of Performance*, edited by Marvin and Ruth Thompson. Newark: University of Delaware Press, 228–49. Clayton argues that "This *Romeo and Juliet* was a certain though unacknowledged adaptation, with the script seemingly as heavily ideologized with supertext as is easily possible without rewriting the script." (232). In more general terms, Clayton raises the questions regarding the producer's and performers' responsibilities to the playwright, the script, the audience(s), "the best interests of society," etc., and distinguishes between an "exploitation production" and an "alienation production" (234ff.).

19. Printed editions of the plays are another matter. Eighteenth-century acting editions often included passages cut in performance but market them with quotation marks or inverted commas.

20. The production was staged at the Khan Theater in Jerusalem in conjunction with a Palestinian group from Ram'allah. The director for the Hebrew part (Capulets) was Eran Baniel; for the Palestinian part (Montagues), Fuad Awad. I am grateful to Professor Avram Oz of the University of Haifa for this information.

21. See "Putting a New Slant on 'Romeo and Juliet.'" 1999. *The Washington Post*, 24 January, C7.

22. Compare Wimsatt, William K. 1954. "The Concrete Universal." In *The Verbal Icon*. Lexington: University of Kentucky Press, 69–83; and Worthen 1997, 65: "Yet while modern dress potentially narrows the play's frame of reference, it also universalizes it: Shakespeare was really writing about *us* all along."

## GLENNIS BYRON ON *ROMEO AND JULIET*: REMADE AND RECONTEXTUALIZED

While *Hamlet* is generally considered to be the most frequently appropriated, quoted and recontextualized of Shakespeare's plays within popular culture, *Romeo and Juliet* certainly runs a close second. "Each generation rewrites Shakespeare for its own purposes," R. S. White notes, and the effectiveness of *Romeo and Juliet* "must largely derive from its capacity for recontextualisation" (White 2001: 3). "The phrase 'Romeo and Juliet,'" White adds,

has become proverbial, two names fused into a single concept signifying a certain kind of love and a certain kind of tragic destiny. How often do we see newspaper headlines like "Romeo and Juliet in Belfast," "Romeo and Juliet in Bosnia," "Romeo and Juliet double teenage suicide"? They refer to young lovers from "different sides of the tracks," divided by the families who represent warring religious or ethnic groups or who disapprove for other reasons of their children's choices in love. They die for their love, either as a result of social persecution or in acts of self-destruction.

(White 2001: 2)

The ways in which the phrase "Romeo and Juliet," or alternatively "star-crossed lovers," is appropriated by the media suggest a further possible refinement to White's assessment. The *San Francisco Chronicle* for May 15, 2005, for example, contained the following news report:

Bethlehem's star-crossed lovers
    Christian girl runs off with young Muslim—Vatican, U.S., Palestinian president intervene after street violence erupts.
    A love feud straight out of "Romeo and Juliet" has erupted in the West Bank over the clandestine romance of a 16-year-old Christian schoolgirl and a wealthy Muslim eight years her senior.

(Kalman 2005)

Similarly, a BBC news report from February 28, 2007, announces:

Star-crossed lovers quit West Bank
    She is a 26-year-old Jewish Israeli. Her name is Jasmine Avissar. He is a 27-year-old Palestinian Muslim, Osama Zaatar. . . .
    "Our marriage was a human thing. We just fell in love," says Jasmine. "The society around us is making it political."

In Shakespeare's play, "A pair of star-crossed lovers take their life" (Prologue: 6). To be a contemporary Romeo and Juliet, these news stories suggest, such drastic measures are quite unnecessary. The focus is instead on conflict, on the "ancient grudge" (Prologue: 3) and, as the second example most clearly suggests, on the autonomy of desire, on a love that, like the love ultimately valorized in the play, is seen as intensely personal, something that transcends the public and the political: "We just fell in love. . . . The society around us is making it political."

The feud is also, of course, central to Shakespeare's play, and its importance stressed by the way the play begins with the fight between servants of the two opposing families and concludes with the scene in which peace is made between the families. But while the feud in Shakespeare's play seems motiveless, the reason for the "ancient grudge" unknown, modern rewritings often politicize the play far more overtly and focus on what seems particularly threatening in the modern world—most frequently the clash between different ethnic group or religions.

Even in adaptations that remain relatively true to source and include tragic death, the feud's the thing. In the 1960s, the best-known film adaptations of *Romeo and Juliet* began to appropriate the story in order to explore social problems: *West Side Story* (1961) replaced the Montagues and Capulets with feuding gangs; Franco Zeffirelli's *Romeo and Juliet* (1968) targeted a generation unwillingly caught up in a war initiated by their parents; and, more recently, Baz Luhrmann's *Romeo + Juliet* (1997) updated the conflict and rescripted Shakespeare's feud to offer an attack on corrupt multinational corporations. For all these political rewritings of the play, however, there has also been an equal impulse to simplify, sentimentalize, and commodify the story of the star-crossed lovers, an impulse particularly evident in the way in which writers of popular romance fiction have appropriated *Romeo and Juliet*. . . .

The "Romance Writers of America" association sets out the two basic elements necessary in the romance genre as follows:

A Central Love Story: In a romance novel, the main plot centers around two individuals falling in love and struggling to make the relationship work. A writer can include as many subplots as he/she wants as long as the relationship conflict is the main focus story.

An Emotionally Satisfying and Optimistic Ending: Romance novels are based on the idea of an innate emotional justice—the notion that good people in the world are rewarded and evil people are punished. In a romance, the lovers who risk and struggle for each other and their relationship are rewarded with emotional justice and unconditional love.

(Romance Writers of America 2007)

Given these second guidelines, *Romeo and Juliet* would at first glance appear an unlikely narrative to interest writers of romance. However, as the story has been transformed in the popular imagination, with the downplaying of death and the foregrounding of conflict, *Romeo and Juliet* has in fact proven eminently amenable to appropriation by popular romance fiction. "The barrier drives the romance novel," Pamela Regis argues, and "more than the marriage" is at stake (Regis 2003: 32). Romance novelists find the feud of Shakespeare's play usefully fulfils the function of this barrier although their appropriations do not usually extend far beyond a simple borrowing of this basic plot element and the use of either the names of the characters, or the shorthand term "star-crossed lovers." . . .

If, as White suggests, the effectiveness of *Romeo and Juliet* stems largely from its capacity for recontextualization, much the same argument is offered to account for the enduring popularity of the vampire. In Nina Auerbach's oft-quoted words, "every age embraces the vampire it needs" (Auerbach 1995: 145). Recent years have seen the vampire quite literally embraced with the growth of a massive vampire romance industry, now generally considered to be the most popular subgenre of paranormal romance. . . .

Shakespeare's Romeo may not fit easily into the category of dangerous man, but *Romeo and Juliet* has nevertheless been so frequently appropriated in vampire romance as to have become a convention, part of the genre competence demanded of the readers. The conflict provided by the feud provides a perfect template for the problems encountered in romances between vampire and werewolf or vampire and human, the two most common couplings. Vampires are usually male, but in the case of vampire-werewolf relationships, since the werewolf is the epitome of the alpha male, women assume the vampiric role, often metaphorically somewhat defanged and transformed to what can only be described as the feisty cuteness so often associated with heroines of romance fiction. . . .

In 1997, an excerpt from *Romeo and Juliet* appeared in John Richard Stephens's *Vampires, Wine and Roses*, an anthology of vampire literature. While the play may seem to have enough in the way of apparently vampiric language and imagery to claim a place in such an anthology, there is nevertheless something anachronistic about its inclusion. In looking to explain a Romeo who "locks fair daylight out, / And makes himself an artifical night" (1.2: 136–37) or a Juliet who describes him "as one dead" (3.4: 56), it would probably be more useful to consult Robert Burton's *Anatomy of Melancholy* (1621) than vampire mythology. Lawrence Schimel's brief story of a vampire Romeo and his human Juliet, "Swear Not By The Moon," makes the point clear. This Juliet plans to kill herself, unable to contemplate life as a vampire with her lover, and taking his dagger from the table she clutches it to her body:

> Romeo murmured as she left his side, and half-opened his eyes to watch her pale form walk to the window and stand before the curtains. She opened them.
>
> Romeo jerked upright. "What light through yonder window breaks?" he cried. "Art thou mad?"
>
> (Schimel 1994: 193)

As Schimel's ludicrous rewriting of the play as vampire story demonstrates, the language and imagery of *Romeo and Juliet* may occasionally duplicate those later found in vampire fictions, but they belong to entirely different systems of representation. To apply the term "Gothic" to Shakespeare's play would be to drain an already threatened term of any meaning whatsoever. Nevertheless, as the vampire infected popular romances during the late twentieth century, so vampire fictions were by no means immune to the contagion of romance, and the number of vampire stories that have appropriated *Romeo and Juliet* suggests some transformation has occurred in the traditional vampire that now allows this figure and the equally iconic star-crossed lovers to merge together with apparent ease.

# Works by William Shakespeare

*Henry VI, Part 1*, circa 1589–1592.

*Henry VI, Part 2*, circa 1590–1592.

*Henry VI, Part 3*, circa 1590–1592.

*Richard III*, circa 1591–1592.

*The Comedy of Errors*, circa 1592–1594.

*Venus and Adonis*, 1593.

*Titus Andronicus*, 1594.

*The Taming of the Shrew*, 1594.

*The Two Gentlemen of Verona*, 1594.

*The Rape of Lucrece*, 1594.

*Love's Labour's Lost*, circa 1594–1595.

*King John*, circa 1594–1596.

*Richard II*, circa 1595.

*Romeo and Juliet*, circa 1595–1596.

*A Midsummer Night's Dream*, circa 1595–1596.

*The Merchant of Venice*, circa 1596–1597.

*Henry IV, Part 1*, circa 1596–1597.

*Henry IV, Part 2*, circa 1597.

*The Merry Wives of Windsor*, 1597.

*Much Ado about Nothing*, circa 1598–99.

*Henry V*, 1599.

*Julius Caesar*, 1599.

*As You Like It*, circa 1599–1600.

*Hamlet*, circa 1600–1601.

*The Phoenix and the Turtle*, 1601.

*Twelfth Night*, circa 1601–1602.

*Troilus and Cressida*, 1601–1602.

*All's Well That Ends Well*, 1602–1603.

*Measure for Measure*, 1604.

*Othello*, 1604.

*King Lear*, 1606.

*Timon of Athens*, 1605–1608.

*Macbeth*, 1606.

*Antony and Cleopatra*, 1606–1607.

*Pericles*, circa 1607–1608.

*Coriolanus*, circa 1607–1608.

*Cymbeline*, 1609.

Sonnets, 1609.

*The Winter's Tale*, 1611.

*The Tempest*, 1611.

*Henry VIII*, 1613.

*The Two Noble Kinsmen*, 1613.

Annotated Bibliography

Bradley, A. C. *Shakespearean Tragedy: Hamlet, Othello, King Lear, Macbeth.* Cleveland and New York: The World Publishing Company, 1904.

For the first decades of the twentieth century, this collection of essays by the preeminent British scholar and teacher A. C. Bradley was an essential component of any academic study of Shakespeare. Although the definition and use of the term *tragedy* has been evolving for centuries, Bradley makes clear the fundamentals of the tragic Shakespearean sense of life. Since the concept has been altered and compromised in contemporary culture—"tragedy" is used indiscriminatingly to describe disasters, calamities, and any random mishap—it is useful to know the classical meanings of the term.

Burt, Richard, ed. *Shakespeare After Mass Media.* New York: Palgrave, 2002.

This collection of essays focuses on the evolution of electronic publishing, mass media, "mass culture" versus "popular culture," and the present-day use of Shakespeare in all forms of mass media—film, video, television, and e-books. The first group of essays examines theoretical issues concerning the cultural authority Shakespeare has held for centuries, while the second group takes up specific adaptations of Shakespeare in mass-media contexts, including business-marketing strategies.

Dean, Leonard F. *Shakespeare: Modern Essays in Criticism,* revised edition. New York: Oxford University Press, 1967.

Although this volume was published more than 40 years ago, it presents the views of some of the most influential Shakespearean scholars and literary critics of the last century. Thirty essays cover most of the plays and discuss the important thematic issues, stagecraft, poetic language, the Elizabethan theater, and Renaissance history and culture.

Drakakis, John, and Dale Townshend, eds. *Gothic Shakespeares.* New York: Routledge, 2008.

Shakespeare's plays memorably include the presence of ghosts and witches, hints of the paranormal, and moments of anxiety and suspense—all components of the gothic sensibility. This volume examines the relationship between Shakespeare and the gothic tradition, particularly the ways that writers in the gothic genre have adapted Shakespeare to their purposes. Writers discussed include Mary Shelley, Horace Walpole, Ann Radcliffe, and Matthew Lewis.

Fisher, Jerilyn, and Ellen S. Silber, eds. *Women in Literature: Reading Through the Lens of Gender*. Westport, Conn., and London: Greenwood Press, 2003.

This volume provides dozens of brief essays examining the presence of women in world literature. The essays are easy to understand and provide a good introduction to the study of literature. The essay on *Romeo and Juliet* emphasizes the strength of character developed and displayed by both Romeo and Juliet as they face the impediments of parental and societal expectations.

Garber, Marjorie. *Shakespeare and Modern Culture*. New York: Pantheon Books, 2008.

Marjorie Garber is a prolific author and celebrated teacher with an impressively wide range of interests and areas of expertise. At the same time, her writing is sufficiently accessible and interesting to be suitable reading for curious students at all but the most introductory level of study. An author of several books on Shakespeare, her focus in this volume is on how "Shakespeare makes modern culture and modern culture makes Shakespeare" (xii). In her introduction, she reminds the reader that the genius of Shakespeare is so enduring and universal that his plays always seem to have contemporary meaning in whatever era he is being read. Shakespeare's influence is so profound that readers in all generations find themselves thinking about meaning, value, and character in terms that seem to emanate from their own culture but whose origins can be traced to one or many of the plays. Garber provides many illuminating details from the current political and cultural context. Garber speculates about what he might have learned had he read them. The volume includes more than 50 illustrations. A chapter is devoted to each of the following plays: *The Tempest, Romeo and Juliet, Coriolanus, Macbeth, Richard III, The Merchant of Venice, Othello, Henry V, Hamlet,* and *King Lear.* The volume includes more than 50 illustrations.

Hunt, Maurice, ed. *Approaches to Teaching Shakespeare's "Romeo and Juliet."* New York: The Modern Language Association of America, 2000.

This volume is one of many in the Approaches to Teaching series and is written mainly by educators for teachers of high school and college literature classes. It has value for students as well, especially those engaged in the larger cultural and psychological issues raised by the plays. Most of the essays deal with the classic version of the play, but there are also helpful discussions about the many contemporary adaptations. One essay deals with the social tragedy of adolescent suicide and the approaches to discussing the separate decision of Romeo and Juliet to take their own lives.

Kermode, Frank, ed. *Four Centuries of Shakespearean Criticism.* New York: Avon Book Division, The Hearst Corporation, 1965.

Kermode introduces this ambitious collection of diverse essays by reminding the reader that only the Bible has attracted more attention and generated more dispute over interpretation than the plays of Shakespeare. The critical tradition was, at the time of this volume's publication, almost four centuries old. Representative commentary, beginning with reviews by the earliest contemporary critics, is included. Some of the critics are themselves key names from the Western literary tradition, authors such as Samuel Johnson, John Milton, John Keats, Ralph Waldo Emerson, Herman Melville, W. H. Auden, and others.

Kliman, Bernice W., and Rick J. Santos, eds. *Latin American Shakespeares.* Madison and Teaneck, N.J.: Fairleigh Dickinson University Press, 2005.

This volume of essays examines different ways that Shakespeare has "infiltrated" Latin America, looking, in particular, at the countries where the Shakespearean presence in the culture is strongest (Brazil, Mexico, and Argentina) and the weakest (Bolivia and Paraguay). A strong cultural resistance to being taken over by American and Western influences has resulted in fascinating adaptations of individual plays and new scholarship. The volume has three sections: Shakespeare read and discussed; Shakespeare on stage; and Shakespeare in film adaptations. An exceptionally long bibliography is invaluable for students interested in Shakespeare and multiculturalism.

Massai, Sonia, ed. *World-Wide Shakespeares: Local Appropriations in Film and Performance.* London and New York: Routledge, 2005.

Inspired by a seminar on "Critical and Creative Appropriations of Shakespeare," the contributors to this collection of essays examine the ways in which Shakespeare's plays have become "globalized"; that is, with easier access to centers of culture and efficient methods of bringing cultural products to outlying areas, Shakespeare has become familiar to many of the world's people. The editor asserts that the rise in the number and kind of Shakespearean appropriations around the world and the spread of these appropriations into mass culture has resulted in Shakespeare becoming a kind of Western icon and/or brand name. These writers, concerned about cultural translations, look at a diversity of geographical and cultural localities to see whether these "consumable" Shakespeare "products" are having the effect of imposing Western values on non-Western cultures. This volume is most appropriate for advanced students of both Shakespeare and multiculturalism.

Occhiogrosso, Frank, ed. *Shakespeare in Performance: A Collection of Essays.* Newark: University of Delaware Press; London: Associated University Presses, 2003.

Shakespeare performance studies has included stage history, details of the physical performance site or playhouse, the staging of the plays in the Elizabethan period, and attention to the details of performance, and the actual work of the actors, directors, and set designers. This volume amplifies these studies and encourages readers to view Shakespeare's work not as a fixed and static product but as an evolving and unstable entity.

Porter, Joseph A. *Critical Essays on Shakespeare's "Romeo and Juliet."* New York: G. K. Hall & Co., 1997.

This collection of essays has three areas of focus: the importance of the character of Mercutio; new ways of looking at Shakespeare using the recent insights about gender and sexuality; and a look at Shakespeare at work, examining his rewritings and the separate versions of the play. As with most Shakespearean criticism, these essays focus on both the timelessness of the human emotions and conflicts dramatized in the play as well as the specific historical conditions and norms of cultural behavior and expectation unique to the particular characters.

# Contributors

**Harold Bloom** is Sterling Professor of the Humanities at Yale University. Educated at Cornell and Yale universities, he is the author of more than 30 books, including *Shelley's Mythmaking* (1959), *The Visionary Company* (1961), *Blake's Apocalypse* (1963), *Yeats* (1970), *The Anxiety of Influence* (1973), *A Map of Misreading* (1975), *Kabbalah and Criticism* (1975), *Agon: Toward a Theory of Revisionism* (1982), *The American Religion* (1992), *The Western Canon* (1994), *Omens of Millennium: The Gnosis of Angels, Dreams, and Resurrection* (1996), *Shakespeare: The Invention of the Human* (1998), *How to Read and Why* (2000), *Genius: A Mosaic of One Hundred Exemplary Creative Minds* (2002), *Hamlet: Poem Unlimited* (2003), *Where Shall Wisdom Be Found?* (2004), and *Jesus and Yahweh: The Names Divine* (2005). In addition, he is the author of hundreds of articles, reviews, and editorial introductions. In 1999, Professor Bloom received the American Academy of Arts and Letters' Gold Medal for Criticism. He has also received the International Prize of Catalonia, the Alfonso Reyes Prize of Mexico, and the Hans Christian Andersen Bicentennial Prize of Denmark.

**A. C. Bradley** was a prominent British early twentieth-century literary critic most celebrated for his scholarship on Shakespeare. He taught literature at University College at Liverpool and at Glasgow and Oxford universities.

**Harry Levin** was professor of comparative literature at Harvard. He published many books and essays of literary criticism, including *James Joyce* (1941) and *The Question of Hamlet* (1959). His last publications were *Shakespeare and the Revolution of the Times* (1976), *Memories of Moderns* (1980), and *Playboys and Killjoys: Essays on the Theory and Practice of Comedy* (1988).

**Sara Munson Deats** teaches in the department of English at the University of South Florida where she is also a Distinguished

University Professor. She is the author of *Sex, Gender, and Desire in the Plays of Christopher Marlowe*, and her many articles on Shakespeare and Marlowe have appeared in *Theatre Journal* and *Literature/Film Quarterly*.

**Arthur F. Kinney** is the Thomas W. Copeland Professor of Literary History at the University of Massachusetts at Amherst where is also the director of the Massachusetts Center for Renaissance Studies. He is the author of *Renaissance Drama: An Anthology of Plays and Entertainments* (1999) and edited *The Cambridge Companion to English Literature, 1500–1600* (2000). He was co-editor of *Tudor England: An Encyclopedia* (2000).

**Stephen M. Buhler** teaches in the English department at the University of Nebraska at Lincoln. He is the author of *Shakespeare in the Cinema: Ocular Proof*, and has also published work on Milton and Spenser. His main area of interest is the interface between literary culture and the performing arts.

**Peter S. Donaldson** is a professor in the literature department at the Massachusetts Institute of Technology, where he also directs the Shakespeare Electronic Archive. He has written several articles about Shakespeare and film and is the author of *Machiavelli and Mystery of State* and *Shakespearean Films/ Shakespearian Directors*.

**Leslie Broder** is a high school teacher of literature and language arts in Bellmore, New York, and a teacher of English as a second language to college students. Her ongoing interests include issues of gender and sexuality in Victorian and twentieth-century literature.

**Jay L. Halio** teaches English at the University of Delaware. He has published as author or editor more than 20 books on Shakespeare and contemporary fiction including editions of *Macbeth, The Merchant of Venice,* and *King Lear*.

**Glennis Byron** teaches English studies at the University of Stirling and directs the master's program in the gothic imagination. She has published several articles on the gothic and is currently working on the concept of a global gothic.

Acknowledgments

A. C. Bradley, excerpts from "The Substance of Shakespearean Tragedy," from *Shakespearean Tragedy*, pp. 14–40. Published by World Publishing Company/Meridian Books. Copyright © 1904, 1963.

Harry Levin, excerpts from "Form and Formality in *Romeo and Juliet*," *Shakespeare Quarterly*, vol. 11, no. 1 (1960): 3–11. Copyright © 1960 Folger Shakespeare Library. Reprinted with permission of the Johns Hopkins University Press.

Sara Munson Deats, excerpts from "Teaching *Romeo and Juliet* as a Tragedy of the Generation Gap and of Teenage Suicide," from *Approaches to Teaching Shakespeare's "Romeo and Juliet,"* pp. 108–14. Copyright © 2000 by and reprinted by permission of the Modern Language Association of America.

Arthur F. Kinney, excerpts from "Authority in *Romeo and Juliet*," from *Approaches to Teaching Shakespeare's "Romeo and Juliet,"* pp. 29–36. Copyright © 2000 by and reprinted by permission of the Modern Language Association of America.

Stephen M. Buhler, excerpts from "Reviving Juliet, Repackaging Romeo: Transformations of Character in Pop and Post-Pop Music," from *Shakespeare after Mass Media*, edited by Richard Burt, pp. 243–64. Copyright © 2002 Richard Burt. Reproduced with permission of Palgrave Macmillan.

Peter S. Donaldson, excerpts from "'In Fair Verona': Media, Spectacle, and Performance in *William Shakespeare's Romeo + Juliet*," from *Shakespeare after Mass Media*, edited by Richard Burt, pp. 59–82. Copyright © 2002 Richard Burt. Reproduced with permission of Palgrave Macmillan.

Lesley Broder, excerpts from "Heroism Against the Odds: William Shakespeare's *Romeo and Juliet*," from *Women in*

Every effort has been made to contact the owners of copyrighted material and secure copyright permission. Articles appearing in this volume generally appear much as they did in their original publication with few or no editorial changes. In some cases, foreign language text has been removed from the original essay. Those interested in locating the original source will find the information cited above.

# Index